VICTIMS
OF DEAD MAN
WALKING

VICTIMS OF DEAD MAN WALKING

DETECTIVE MICHAEL L. VARNADO
AND D. P. SMITH

PELICAN PUBLISHING COMPANY
Gretna 2003

*The word "Pelican" and the depiction of a pelican are trademarks
of Pelican Publishing Company, Inc., and are registered
in the U.S. Patent and Trademark Office.*

Library of Congress Cataloging-in-Publication Data

Varnado, Michael L., 1953-
 Victims of dead man walking / detective Michael L. Varnado and D.P. Smith.
  p. cm.
 ISBN 1-58980-156-3 (hardcover : alk. paper)
 1. Hathaway, Faith Colleen, 1961-1980. 2. Murder—Louisiana—Case studies.
3. Murder—Investigation—Louisiana—Case studies. 4. Trials (Murder)—
Louisiana—Case studies. 5. Murders—Louisiana—Case studies. 6. Willie,
Robert Lee. 7. Vaccaro, Joe. 8. Death row inmates—Louisiana—Case studies.
9. Capital punishment—Louisiana—Case studies. I. Smith, Daniel P., 1955-
II. Title.
 HV6533.L8 V37 2003
 364.15'23'09763—dc21

                                        2003005371

Scripture taken from the *Holy Bible, New International Version* ®. Copyright ©
1973, 1978, 1984 by International Bible Society. Used by permission of
Zondervan Publishing House. All rights reserved.

The "NIV" and "New International Version" trademarks are registered in the
United States Patent and Trademark Office by International Bible Society. Use
of either trademark requires the permission of International Bible Society.

Printed in the United States of America

Published by Pelican Publishing Company, Inc.
1000 Burmaster Street, Gretna, Louisiana 70053

For all the forgotten victims and those who bear the scars of loss long after the headlines have faded

CONTENTS

ACKNOWLEDGMENTS

I want to thank the following people: The late Sheriff Willie Jay Blair for believing in me even though I was young and green. Judge Hillary J. Crain for pointing his finger (which looked a mile long) in my face when I was a teenager and telling me to straighten up and fly right. Jerry Brumfield for taking me under his wing and teaching me how to be a good deputy sheriff those many years ago. D.A. Walter Reed for setting a standard of excellence that all prosecutors should emulate. Also, Lewis V. Murray III, a great prosecutor and friend, and Annie Rose Bickham. Joanne Smith at the Clerk's Office for all her help. Judge Ray Childress. Court Clerk Johnny Crain. Major league thanks to Steve, Paula, Ms. Moggie, and Ms. Loretta at The *Era-Leader*. Thanks also to Dr. Larry Stack.

I especially want to thank my family. My daughter, Jade, for turning out so well even though I was not always around to help. My daughter, Jessica. My two boys, Josh and JoJo. My wonderful wife, Debbie. I love you all.

Thanks also to the entire town of Franklinton and all of Washington Parish for making this a perfect place to raise a family—a place where Jesus is Lord of all.

Finally, I want to thank the good Lord for helping me find the truth and for standing beside me through some very tough times. He always guided my sword.   —M. L. V.

"Do you want to be free from fear of the one in authority? Then do what is right and he will commend you. For he is God's servant to do you good. But if you do wrong, be afraid, for he does not bear the sword for nothing. He is God's servant, an agent of wrath to bring punishment on the wrongdoer."

Romans 13:3b-4

"A voice is heard in Ramah, weeping and great mourning, Rachel weeping for her children, and refusing to be comforted, because they are no more."

Matthew 2:18

Author's Note

This is a true story. The events described in this book are based on my own personal experiences in connection with the investigation of the brutal rape and murder of Faith Hathaway by Robert Lee Willie and Joe Vaccaro, as well as interviews with many of the participants, the voluminous trial transcripts, other official records and media accounts of the crimes that shocked a community.

It is perhaps not surprising that co-defendants in criminal cases often tell law enforcement officials slightly different versions of what really happened. The crimes portrayed in this book are no exception. In most instances, I have attempted to sift through the conflicting stories and have portrayed what appeared to be the most reasonable scenario. In some instances, I have merely set forth the conflicting versions, leaving it up to the reader to decide which version, combination of versions, or neither version more nearly reflects reality. In all cases where facts are in dispute, I have tried to note the existence of that uncertainty.

Much of the dialogue appearing in this book comes directly from the trial transcripts, official records and other sources I believe to be reasonably trustworthy. The rest represents my best effort to accurately recreate scenes at which there were no cameras, recording devices, or (in some cases) credible surviving witnesses.

I would like to make one additional comment with respect to the crime scene photographs that are included in this book.

They are obviously extremely graphic in nature. If a picture is worth a thousand words, then these photographs speak volumes as to the horrific brutality of the rape and murder of Faith Hathaway. These photographs would not have been included in this book, however, without the express approval and support of Faith's mother, Elizabeth Harvey. Mrs. Harvey noted that after Faith's murder, people often hesitated to even say Faith's name, as if she had never existed. Instead, all the attention was focused on Robert Lee Willie—his rights, his last visit, his last meal, his last minutes on earth. Mrs. Harvey felt that it was important to include the crime scene photos "to show what Faith's last of everything was like."

PROLOGUE

Death Row, Louisiana State Penitentiary, Angola, Louisiana. October 1984. It is nearly midnight and, except for the occasional clanking of metal on metal somewhere in the distant bowels of the prison, the tier is quiet. Through the barred, tilt-in windows opposite the cells and separated from them by a hallway six feet wide, Robert Lee Willie can see the full moon as it rises over the Tunica Hills in the distance. It is a cool night and the guards have left the windows open on the tier. Standing perfectly still and pressing his face against the cool steel of the bars of his cell, Willie can feel a slight breeze on his face. He closes his eyes and breathes in deeply, tasting the perfume of the night—a mixture of mowed grass and the nearby Mississippi River.

He turns and sits on his bunk, picking up a crumpled letter lying there. He unfolds the letter, which he has already read a number of times, and studies it once again. A nun from New Orleans says she is willing to come to Death Row and visit him, perhaps even be his spiritual adviser as he awaits his appointment with the executioner.

Willie takes a sheet of paper and a pencil from the small table beside him. "What the hell," he thinks. "Why not?"

Just past midnight, December 28, 1984. I have just watched Robert Lee Willie die. As the seven other witnesses and I file out of the witness room adjacent to Angola's death chamber and into the crisp night air, I have no reason to doubt that the final word has been written and the book closed on the short, violent life of Robert Lee Willie. I am wrong.

In 1993, the New Orleans nun who served as spiritual adviser to Willie publishes a book that chronicles her experiences with Willie and Elmo Patrick Sonnier, another Louisiana Death Row inmate. Her book is a full-frontal assault on the legitimacy of the death penalty.

The terror and death that Robert Lee Willie visited on Faith Colleen Hathaway, an innocent eighteen-year-old girl from a small town in St. Tammany Parish, and the loss of innocence that reverberated throughout nearby Washington Parish come bubbling to the surface once again. Almost a decade after Robert Lee Willie's death in the electric chair, old wounds are ripped open once again.

Surely, the family and friends of Faith Hathaway deserve some small portion of peace—a peace that can only be found in having Robert Willie pass forever from the public arena where in death, in the eyes of some, he has attained the status of victim. I think that surely the nun's 1993 book represents the final gasp for Robert Lee Willie's undeserved notoriety. Again, I am wrong.

In 1995, fully fifteen years since that bright spring morning in late May 1980 when eighteen-year-old Faith Hathaway's body lay butchered deep in the woods of Fricke's Cave, crowds of eager movie fans sit transfixed in movie theatres across the country. On a flickering screen, a handsome young man with a goatee dressed in a plain white tee shirt, his dark hair slicked back, sits talking through the screen of a Death Row visitor's room to a beautiful young nun, her large eyes filled with love and compassion for him. The movie, *Dead Man Walking*, based on Sister Helen Prejean's book of the same name, kindles the debate over the death penalty like no other film before or since has done.

In the movie *Dead Man Walking*, the essential details of the life of the young girl who is murdered are directly echoed in the too-short life of Faith Hathaway, who died at the hands of Robert Lee Willie. Sean Penn in the role of Matthew Poncelet, a Death

Row inmate in the Louisiana State Penitentiary at Angola, is an eerily near-perfect, mirror image of Robert Lee Willie.

At the 1995 Academy Awards, Susan Sarandon in her acceptance speech for Best Actress praised Sister Helen Prejean and her work in the fight against the death penalty in America, and the crowd applauded for the nun who was now a celebrity. No word was spoken about the victims of murder. No word was spoken about Faith Hathaway who was then more than fifteen years in her grave. No word was spoken of the lives of her parents who were decimated by the crimes committed by Robert Lee Willie. No one remembered or seemed to care about a poor young girl named Faith Colleen Hathaway. Although innocent of any crime, she had been slaughtered like an animal in the woods and now her death had become mere fodder for those with a political agenda to abolish the death penalty.

Although millions of people worldwide have read Helen Prejean's book, *Dead Man Walking: An Eyewitness Account of the Death Penalty in the United States,* or have seen the movie based on it, very few know the true story of the real-life *Dead Man Walking,* Robert Lee Willie. Sadly, even fewer know anything of his innocent victim, Faith Hathaway.

I am in a unique position to write this book. I discovered Faith Hathaway's battered body deep in the woods outside Franklinton, Louisiana, one week after her murder, after earlier attempts to locate her body had failed and the search had been called off. As chief investigator for the District Attorney's Office, I also headed the investigation that led to the conviction of Robert Lee Willie and his accomplice, Joe Vaccaro. There were eight official witnesses to Robert Lee Willie's execution. As portrayed in the movie *Dead Man Walking,* Helen Prejean was one of the witnesses. I was also a witness to Robert Lee Willie's execution.

I have seen firsthand the savagery that Robert Willie wrought not only on Faith Hathaway, but also on her family, the community at large, and, in the final analysis, even on me. Violent crime, particularly murder, is like a pebble thrown into a lake. One sees the immediate impact, hears the splash, but the ripples continue to flow outward from it, changing the course of the lives of those involved forever.

My goal is straightforward. I want to accurately portray the devastation that Robert Lee Willie left in his violent wake so that readers of this book will never again hear the phrase "Dead Man Walking" without thinking about the innocent young girl murdered by Robert Lee Willie and Joe Vaccaro. Her name was Faith Colleen Hathaway. She deserves to be remembered.

Dennis Hemby

Covington, Louisiana. 3:20 A.M., May 23, 1978. It will be a couple of hours before dawn breaks in this small town in the southeastern corner of the state—the toe of the boot—not far north of Lake Pontchartrain. Throughout Covington, houses and businesses are dark and families sleep peacefully in their beds. But one small corner of the town is awake and alive with jukebox music, neon and the smell of beer—the Tavern Lounge. Even past 3:00 A.M., the Tavern Lounge, just down an alley from the darkened St. Tammany Parish Courthouse, is brimming with the restless energy of those unable or unwilling to sleep, men who want to drink the night away and who prefer the smoky and raucous atmosphere of a bar to the peace of a bed.

Nineteen-year-old Dennis Hemby sits at the bar, drinking a beer and studying the crowd. He is just shy of six feet tall, but is thin at 165 pounds. His hair is dark and wavy and of medium length. Originally from Puxico, Missouri, he has been living in the Covington area for a while now, staying with his cousin and her husband. Sometimes he sleeps in their mobile home. Other times he bunks in the old bus that sits behind it.

Dennis is wearing a western shirt and a new pair of light tan cowboy boots, which he has borrowed from his cousin's husband, Gary. He has also borrowed Gary's cargo van, which is long and black and has honeycomb mag wheels. There are no seats in the rear of the van, and its carpeted floor is littered with fish and frog gigs and other assorted junk. A small, round bullet hole punctuates the van's rear door on the driver's side.

Dennis closes his eyes and takes a long drink from his long-neck beer. When he opens his eyes, he sees a long-haired, bearded man standing in front of him, grinning. The man's face is heavily pockmarked beneath the beard. "Hey, how's it going?" the man asks, his voice a slurred drawl.

Before Dennis can answer, the man tilts his head to one side. His eyes are slightly unfocused, but Dennis looks across the bar in the direction the man seems to be indicating. "See those two dudes over by the jukebox? They want to buy some weed," he says.

Dennis squints through the smoky haze and sees two men lounging against the far wall by the jukebox. One is small and skinny and has shoulder-length, dirty blonde hair. The other is taller and much more muscular. Dennis takes a final sip of his beer and sets the empty bottle on the bar. "Thanks," he says and eases past the drunk with the beard and the bad skin. He saunters over toward the jukebox and the two men waiting there.

"Hey, what's going on?" Dennis says.

"Not much," the skinny blonde man says. "Just looking to buy a little weed. You wouldn't know where we might get some, would you?"

Hemby nods. "Uh huh, I see." He studies the faces of the two men. "I'm Dennis," he says, holding out the palm of his right hand.

The skinny blonde man looks at Dennis's hand for a moment before slapping it with his own. "I'm Robert Willie," he says. "Most people around here just call me Willie."

Robert Lee Willie, also known as Little Willie and Little John after his father, John Willie, an inmate at Angola, is well known in Frog Alley and the Ozone area of Covington as someone not to be messed with. Although he is small of stature, only five foot six inches and one hundred twenty-five pounds, Robert Lee Willie likes to settle disputes and grudges with violence. Once he broke a broom handle in two and gave one half to a friend, and then they both proceeded to beat another man senseless. Willie was arrested, but he posted a bond of twenty-five dollars and was released from jail. As soon as he was released, he returned to the victim's home, stormed in and hit him in the head with a bottle. Willie was arrested again, and when he stepped out of the police cruiser at the sheriff's office, a knife fell out of his shirt. Indeed, Willie is widely known in the lawless fringe in which he runs as a knife man.

A little over a year before, Robert Lee Willie had pled guilty to burglarizing both the American Legion Hall and Jim's Chicken Town. He and several accomplices had broken into the Legion Hall, located a safe, wheeled it outside and lifted it into the trunk of their car. In the burglary of Jim's Chicken Town, Willie and an accomplice had broken in and stolen money, beer and chewing gum.

After being arrested for these burglaries, Willie was sentenced to three years of hard labor, but the judge suspended his sentence and placed him on probation for three years. Willie failed to report to his probation officer and, for almost five months, he was not heard from. Then, he was arrested again and charged with aggravated battery, carrying a concealed weapon and disturbing the peace. He was released on bond the same day, even though he was in violation of his probation. Eventually, a probation violation warrant was issued, and Willie was picked up and placed in jail. However, he was released from jail after only a short time. Now, five months later, he was in the Tavern Lounge trying to buy dope.

The larger, muscular man standing beside Willie in the Tavern Lounge is quiet. "This here's my cousin, Perry," Willie says. He nods at Dennis.

Dennis looks at his watch, seeing that it will not be long before dawn.

"I might be able to help you out with that weed," he says. "Come on outside with me."

Dennis walks out of the Tavern and into the parking lot followed by Willie and his cousin, Perry. As they stand beside the black cargo van, Willie rubs his finger along the side, feeling the bullet hole. He grins. "How'd this happen?"

Dennis shrugs. "I don't know. It ain't my van."

Dennis opens the driver's side door and hops in, searching for a bag of marijuana hidden under the seat. His fingers find the plastic bag and he holds it up.

"Not here," Willie says. He cocks his head to the left. "See that building over there, down the alley? That's the courthouse where the Sheriff's Department is. Let's go for a ride."

"OK," Dennis says. Willie and his cousin climb into the van.

"Where're we going?" Dennis asks.

"I know a place, down by the river," Willie says.

In a moment, the van spins out of the parking lot and heads out of town through the dark and deserted streets. In the distance, the sky is beginning to lighten from black to a dull gray.

The sun is just coming up as the van pulls to a stop on a dirt road near the Bogue Falaya River. Power lines run overhead. The three men pile out of the van.

As they stand beside the van, Willie rolls a joint. "How much for the weed?" he asks.

"Thirty-five," Dennis says. Willie nods his head in agreement.

As the men smoke, Dennis reaches into the van and pulls out a .38 caliber revolver. He aims at a bottle lying near the riverbank, but does not pull the trigger.

"Hey," Willie says. "Can I see your gun?"

Dennis hesitates, but Willie grins as he takes a long hit of the joint. "Come on, man. I just want to see it," he says. Dennis hands Willie the gun.

Willie turns the large revolver over in his hands, feeling its weight. "Nice," he says. He aims at the same bottle on the riverbank. Then, slowly, his hand moves toward Dennis, stopping as the gun points directly at Dennis's face.

"What the hell?" Dennis says.

"Shut up," Willie says. "Turn around."

He pushes the gun into Dennis's back. "Walk," he says.

They walk down a small hill towards the riverbank. As they near the water, Willie hits Dennis in the back of the head and pushes him into the river. The blow stuns Dennis, and he falls backwards. His mouth fills with river water and he chokes and gasps. Before he can get his bearings, he feels the weight of a body on him, pushing him down, hands grasping his throat.

Willie is smaller than Dennis, but the blow on the head and the suddenness of the attack have leveled the field. They struggle for several minutes, but Willie has the upper hand. As Dennis fights to free himself, Willie gets a headlock on him and succeeds in holding Dennis's head under the water. Dennis thrashes and kicks, desperate now to get a breath, but Willie's grip is tight. Soon the thrashing weakens and then stops entirely. Willie lets go of Dennis, who is now limp in the water. For several minutes, Willie sits on the limp body, resting from the exertion of the fight.

Finally, Willie and his cousin pick Dennis up by the shirt and drag his body to the bank. They wrestle him into the van, get in and start it up. They drive into the woods, where they stop and drag Dennis's lifeless body out and throw it under a tree. Willie reaches into Dennis's pocket and takes out a small bundle of money, which is soaking wet. They cover Dennis's body with sticks and leaves. As they drive away, Willie finds the marijuana hidden under the seat in the van. Later, they will siphon gas out of the van's gas tank and set it afire.

LOUIS WAGNER

Covington, Louisiana. 10:00 P.M., Thursday, June 1, 1978. Scarcely a week has passed since Dennis Hemby walked out of the Tavern Lounge with Robert Lee Willie and disappeared into the night without a trace. Just down the alley from the Tavern Lounge, Sergeant Louis H. Wagner III stretches as he walks into the radio room of the St. Tammany Parish Sheriff's Office and grins at Lieutenant D.V. Chatellier.

"I'm going home and change into my civvies," he tells Chatellier. "Donna's asleep, I guess, but at least I can check on her and give her a hug." Louis Wagner's wife, Donna Wagner, is three months pregnant, expecting their second child.

"How're your folks doing?" Chatellier asks.

Louis laughs and slaps Chatellier on the shoulder. "What do you think? They can't wait to be grandparents again."

Only twenty-six years old, Louis Wagner has become a valuable member of the St. Tammany force, working narcotics as well as handling the day-to-day matters that come into the office.

"I think I'll ride around for a while and see if I can find any trace of those boys who escaped this morning," Louis says. At 7:00 o'clock that morning, four inmates had escaped and had been on the loose all day. Although the heat and drought of summer usually come early in southern Louisiana, recent rains had been so heavy that all of the back roads around Covington had become muddy and almost impassable. Louis figured that his Bronco would be the perfect vehicle to hunt for the four

22

escapees in the remote, wooded areas outside of town, where they would be most likely to hide.

"It's awfully late, Louis," Chatellier says. "Haven't you had enough police work for one day? Go on home and stay put with that pretty young wife of yours, why don't you? Those boys won't get far in the dark. We'll find them tomorrow."

Louis grins and shakes his head. "Nope. I'm going to look for them before they have a chance to get too far away," he says. "Besides, I thought I might drive around later and do a little surveillance on some of our local druggies."

Wagner waves over his shoulder as he heads out the door and into the night.

Lieutenant Chatellier is still on duty at 1:22 A.M., when Sergeant Wagner walks back into the radio room. "Any luck on those escapees?" he asks.

"Nope," Louis says. "Not a bit, but I bet they're not far away. We'll probably get them tomorrow."

"It's already tomorrow," Chatellier says with a grin. "Aren't you ready to call it a day yet?"

"Yeah, almost," Louis says. "First, though, could you get the operator to call Covington PD? There are four guys just down the alley drinking on the street in front of the Tavern Lounge."

"Sure thing, Louis," Chatellier says.

"I'm out of here," Louis says.

Chatellier walks out with Louis Wagner. The night is warm and pleasant, and they chat briefly beside Louis's Bronco, unaware that the characters that Louis had spotted drinking on the street are waiting nearby.

Four scraggly boys in their early twenties stand by two beat up cars in the parking lot of the Tavern Lounge waiting for Louis Wagner. One of them is Robert Lee Willie.

When Louis gets into his Bronco and pulls away from the Sheriff's Office, two of the boys jump into an old brown Cutlass and pull out quickly, followed by Willie and another boy in a white Camaro, its body pockmarked with gray primer spots.

At first, Louis drives slowly down the deserted roads of Covington, his mind on the long day he has just put in. Except for the quick trip home after his regular shift, he has been on the job since early afternoon. His back aches, his head hurts, his eyes are so heavy that everything looks a little blurry. Finally, though, he can get home and get some rest.

The first indication he has that something isn't quite right is the steady beams of the car behind him. When Louis speeds up, the car following him seems to speed up as well. When Louis slows down, the car behind him also slows down. As Louis takes a curve in the road, he sees for the first time that there is a second car directly behind the one following him, and he knows this means trouble.

Louis is used to dealing with thugs and bad characters as a result of his narcotics work. He knows that he has made some enemies among a core of rough young punks who wouldn't give a second thought to attacking anyone who stands in their way, even if that person is a policeman—especially if that person is a policeman. Louis touches his pistol with the fingers of his right hand and eases down on the accelerator as he approaches another curve in the road.

Coming out of the curve, he punches the Bronco and feels the familiar surge of power as the big truck responds and he pulls away from the two cars following him. As the first car negotiates the turn, however, all pretense has now been ripped away. The brown Cutlass roars to life, and within a few moments, it has made up the distance it lost to the Bronco. And it is closing fast. The Camaro is also rocketing down the road just behind the Cutlass.

"If I can just hold on," Louis thinks. "Everything's going to be OK. I just need to hold on," he whispers to himself.

But it is clear that the cars pursuing him are faster than he is. In a screech of tires, the Cutlass lurches sharply to the left and then to the right. It is now in front of him. In another moment, the Camaro whips out in the lane beside the Bronco and pulls directly beside Louis.

Louis glances quickly at the two long-haired men in the car beside him. The one in the passenger seat is only a couple of feet away. If they each stuck their arms out the window, they could touch fingertips. But the long-haired blonde man in the Camaro has something totally different in mind. From his lap, Robert Willie pulls a twelve-gauge shotgun and sticks it out the window, pointing it directly at Louis.

At this moment, the Cutlass begins to slow down and Louis has no choice but to slow down as well. He is boxed in. In a moment, the Cutlass comes to a dead stop and Louis pulls to a stop behind it.

Louis cuts the engine of the Bronco, but before he can get out of the truck, the driver of the Camaro appears at his window. "Get out," he says.

"Y'all know I'm a police officer?" Louis asks.

The man standing beside his truck laughs. "Yeah, I know that. You should have thought about that when you come up in my house," he says.

Louis gets out of his truck and waits, hoping that someone will drive by, although at this time of night on the outskirts of Covington, it is not likely to happen. At that moment, the two men from the Cutlass appear and stand in front of him. One is grinning. The other has a crazed and angry look on his face.

With a grunt, the man with the crazed look throws himself at Louis, hitting him hard with his fist right in the center of his chest. Louis stumbles and falls. As he lies on the pavement, the four men crowd over him. He gets to his knee and then stands, unsure how all of this is going to play out.

"Watch that son of a bitch," one of them says.

"You boys better just get out of here. You're in a lot of trouble," Louis says, wiping his hands on his pants. They just laugh.

The driver of the Camaro shakes his head.

"No. You're the one who's in a lot of trouble," he says. "Move over there." He cocks his head in the direction of the Camaro.

Louis walks over to the Camaro, glancing at Robert Lee Willie, the thin, blonde-haired man who is holding the shotgun on him. He stops and looks directly at the one who had been driving the Camaro. "Every dog has its day," the boy says. "And today is your day."

In that moment, Louis makes his decision.

With a deep breath, he breaks and runs, his feet crunching through the tall grass beside the road. If he can just make it across the road to Brown's Funeral Home, perhaps he can find cover. His heart is beating wildly, its thumping making a deafening roar in his ears. Suddenly, a shot rings out. Louis feels a searing pain in his back. He has been hit.

As he falls, he turns and sees that the boy who had said that today was his day is holding a small silver pistol at shoulder height, a small puff of smoke rising from its barrel.

In the moment before his death, Louis thinks of Donna, who is asleep in their bed just a few miles away. He thinks of his precious little one whom he had kissed goodbye that morning. His last conscious thought is of the child he will never know and who will never know him. "I love you," he whispers. Then he is still.

The one who shot Louis comes up to his body first. "Wow, man! I didn't think I had hit him."

"Well, I believe he's dead," Willie says. He kicks at Louis's body with the toe of his boot. He laughs. "Yeah, he's not moving. He's dead."

As Louis's body lies in the weeds beside the road in front of Brown's Funeral Home, Robert Lee Willie and the other three men jump in their cars and in Louis's Bronco and race away, the screech of their tires shattering the stillness of the night.

After the killing of Louis Wagner in the early morning hours of June 2, 1978, Willie packed his bags and headed for Baton Rouge. Although the authorities knew nothing of Willie's involvement in the murder of Dennis Hemby and Louis Wagner, an arrest warrant was issued for him because he had left the area while still on probation. The Covington Police arrested Willie three months later, but he was released on bond the same day, and the probation warrant was not enforced. Willie was arrested again two weeks later and placed in jail.

Two months later, Willie escaped from the St. Tammany Parish jail. He simply pushed past a guard, made it to the roof of the jail on the third floor and jumped down to the roof of the second floor. From there, he climbed down and escaped. He hurt his ankle when he jumped, though, and after only being on the loose for a day, he called the sheriff's office and turned himself in, believing that his ankle was broken. It turned out that it was only sprained.

On March 28, 1980, Willie's probation expired, and his case was closed. Although it had now been two years since the murders of Dennis Hemby and Sergeant Louis Wagner, there still were no viable leads in Sergeant Wagner's killing, and officially, Dennis Hemby was still classified as a missing person.

As each day passed in the spring of 1980, Robert Lee Willie became more and more emboldened by his success in avoiding prosecution. Except for a short stint in the parish jail, the police had not been able to touch him. Even then, he was able to escape from their pathetic little jail. He was the ultimate outlaw. After all, twice now, he had gotten away with murder. What could stop him now? And why should he stop at anything?

FAITH HATHAWAY AND THE DAWN OF A NEW DECADE

Mandeville, Louisiana. May 20, 1980. It has been an unusual road that has led eighteen-year-old Faith Colleen Hathaway to this special night, one that has taken her from Haiti, the poorest nation in the western hemisphere, to the teeming metropolis of Quayaquil, Ecuador, on the coast of the Pacific Ocean, and now back to her home in Mandeville, Louisiana. Faith is a pretty girl, her hair falling in curls on her shoulders, her nose a button. She is five feet five inches tall and weighs one hundred thirty pounds. She signs her name in a simple girlish cursive. Something of a tomboy, Faith loves horses, swimming and jogging. And books. Her family kids that she never goes anywhere without a book.

Tonight on a school football field filled with students and their friends and family members, Faith sits quietly, dressed in her graduation gown and her mortarboard cap, waiting for her name to be called. She smiles and chats with friends as, one by one, the boys and girls she has walked the halls of Mandeville High School this past year hear their names called and ascend the stage to receive their diplomas. This is Faith's proudest moment, prouder even than the time six years before where, in a local sawdust-filled ring, a twelve-year-old Faith had urged her galloping pony on toward the finish line, and she had won her first barrel race.

Faith was born on December 17, 1961, in Orlando, Florida, to Elizabeth Hathaway and Edwin Ray "Sunny" Hathaway. When Faith was just six months old, Sunny moved out, leaving a young and scared Elizabeth to fend for herself and her infant daughter.

28

Elizabeth poured all of her energies into caring for Faith, but it was often a struggle for the young, single-again mother. Still, Elizabeth was quite pretty, and she had an outgoing personality. When Faith was just a young girl, Elizabeth met and fell in love with a handsome young man named Vernon Harvey.

Vern Harvey was a man's man, a tough Navy veteran of World War II. Still, just as the rugged Vern Harvey had fallen in love with Elizabeth, so he also fell in love with Faith, his rough heart made tender by the little girl who now called him "Daddy."

Elizabeth and Vern married and from that moment, Vernon Harvey became every bit a father to Faith. A few years later, Vernon and Elizabeth Harvey had a daughter of their own together, Lizabeth, and although Lizabeth was nine years younger than Faith, Faith and Lizabeth were as close as sisters could be.

Faith attended Mandeville public schools from the first grade through the ninth grade. Then, in early 1977, Vernon Harvey, a master carpenter, took Elizabeth and his two girls with him to Port-au-Prince, Haiti, where he had a job working on a construction project there. Vernon, Elizabeth, and their two daughters would live in Haiti for the next eighteen months.

For Faith, Port-au-Prince opened up a whole new world of possibilities. Here, more than a thousand miles from the rural back roads of southeastern Louisiana, Faith saw just how exciting the world could be for a girl willing to go out and make her place in it. And Faith lost no time in exploring the exotic wonders of Port-au-Prince.

Faith delighted in mixing with the throngs of dark-skinned Haitians in the crowded marketplaces of Port-au-Prince, listening to the lilt of their Creole French and learning a new way of looking at the world. To her surprise, Faith discovered that she had a gift for languages, and so she was soon exploring the marketplaces on a daily basis in order to practice her increasingly proficient language skills.

In Port-au-Prince, Faith also met and befriended a young girl from Holland, Nora Overwell, whose father was in Haiti, working on a new telephone system for the country. At first, Nora spoke no English and Faith spoke no Dutch, but the two girls became close friends over the eighteen months that the Harveys spent in Haiti, and each girl began to teach the other her native language. When the Harveys left Haiti, Faith and Nora remained in contact, writing long letters to each other. Nora would write to Faith in English and Faith would write to Nora in Dutch, each correcting the other's errors.

In August of 1978, Vern Harvey finished his work in Haiti and took his family to Quayaquil, Ecuador, where he had another construction job. Quayaquil, a city of over 1.5 million people, is located on the coast of Ecuador, overlooking the beautiful harbor and the Pacific Ocean. But it wasn't just the scenic beauty of Quayaquil that attracted Faith. If Haiti opened Faith's eyes to the greatness of the world and all of its wonders, Quayaquil only confirmed for her the excitement that she felt in discovering other cultures, meeting new people and learning new languages. She spoke often with Vernon about her interest in languages and in other cultures, and he encouraged her. He told her of his travels in the Navy, and how he had learned so much and seen so much of the world in that way. Before long, Faith began to consider the possibility of combining her love of country with her love of languages. Vernon had gotten so much from military service. Perhaps, Faith thought, I should consider it for myself.

In late 1978, Faith returned with her family to Mandeville. During her senior year in high school, Faith signed up to join the Army immediately after her graduation, planning to focus on a career in foreign languages. Her recruiter, Sergeant Farris, is here tonight, at her graduation. In a week, he has promised to pick her up and drive her personally to New Orleans for induction into the Army.

At that moment, Faith hears her name being called. She smiles and quickly ascends the stage, her gown held tightly against her legs. She reaches up and touches the coolness of her senior class necklace, which is inscribed *Class of 1980* on one side and *Dawn of a New Decade* on the other. When the necklace had arrived with her graduation invitations, her heart had swelled with pride at what she had accomplished so far and with the excitement of the new life awaiting her.

Faith walks to the center of the stage. All eyes are on her. She knows that her parents and her sister are watching with pride as she takes the diploma and looks into the distance. At this moment, a school photographer takes her picture.

She continues across the stage and makes her way back to her seat and, when the time comes, a cheer goes up, and Faith Hathaway, eighteen years old and one week away from starting a new chapter in her life, throws her cap into the air where it joins those of her classmates. She turns to a friend and smiles. Across the field, Faith spots her parents. She breaks into a run and launches herself at Vern Harvey, jumping into his arms and wrapping her legs around his waist. "I made it! I made it!" she says.

The graduation photograph of Faith Hathaway will be the last one taken of her in life. There will be no pictures of her standing next to her parents before she runs to Sergeant Farris's waiting car and, waving, drives off with him to New Orleans and her induction into the Army. No pictures with her fiancé as she stands smiling and holding her hand up to show off a new diamond engagement ring. No picture of a tired, but proud Faith as she cradles a newborn son or daughter. No picture of Faith with her children or grandchildren. On May 20, 1980, at her high school graduation, Faith stood for the last time in the lens of a camera.

Captured forever were her smiling face, her expectant features, her pride, and the cherished graduation necklace dangling on her chest. And this high school picture, usually relegated to a cedar chest or the bottom of a drawer, replaced by more important and up-to-date photographs, would become the best known picture of her, the one that would define her life. The next time that photographs would be taken of Faith, everything would be horribly different. And it would be these photographs taken by a state police crime scene photographer that would become a central part in the murder trial of the two men who took her life.

THE LAKEFRONT DISCO

New Orleans, Louisiana. 12:15 A.M., May 28, 1980. It is past midnight, but in the French Quarter, the party continues. Jazz drifts from the open doors of bars and small clubs, wafted on the warm breeze blowing off the Gulf and through the narrow streets of the Quarter. The air is pungent with a mixture of beignets, coffee, stale beer and shrimp.

A few miles from the French Quarter, as the clubs and bars give way to warehouses and shuttered buildings, Lake Pontchartrain stretches in dark repose. Moonlight shimmers on its choppy waves as beneath the twin spans of the causeway the black water gently laps against giant pilings. The lake is huge, one of the largest natural lakes on earth—forty miles long and twenty-five miles wide. The causeway over Lake Pontchartrain is the longest over-water bridge in the world.

If you stand on the causeway with New Orleans at your back and look due north, straight across the dark expanse of the causeway, twenty-four miles away lies the town of Mandeville, Louisiana. Only thirty minutes from New Orleans, Mandeville seems a world away.

If New Orleans is Mardi Gras, Bourbon Street, and Jackson Square, then Mandeville is high school football, family picnics, and church outings. On this morning long ago, Mandeville seems peaceful and quiet.

Drive across the causeway from New Orleans to Mandeville, though, and meander through the nearly deserted streets all the way down to Lakeshore Drive. You might find yourself standing in front of a large, white stucco building. This is the Lakefront Disco. From the street or standing in the shadows of the live oaks beside the front entrance, you can hear the sound of music pounding through the walls and spilling out into the darkness. Mixed with the rhythmic sound of the lake, you would be hard pressed to find a more pleasant place. But you would be wrong. The innocence of the small town of Mandeville, Louisiana, is on the verge of being lost forever.

Inside the Lakefront Disco this night is a young woman named Faith Hathaway. She has heard the call of patriotism, of duty and country. Tonight is a night of celebration, a night when everything seems possible, when the future seems to stretch ahead of her for years and years. But evil is here in your midst, and death is nearby and waiting.

The past week has seemed like an eternity to Faith. Was it only last week that she walked the stage and received her diploma? Is it possible that this is really her last evening at home? As Faith celebrates with her friends at the Lakefront Disco, she still cannot believe that later today she will be meeting her recruiting sergeant and preparing for induction into the Army. She is about to embark on a life full of promise, travel and adventure.

Monroe Apartments, Mandeville, Louisiana. 4:45 P.M., May 27, 1980. Faith takes a last look at herself in the mirror. She is dressed in a blue skirt, a blue blouse, and her Mexican-style sandals. As she brushes her hair back into place with her hand, she notices the seven-day wishing ring that her mother had given her. She straightens her senior class necklace, and checks her watch, a Timex with a blue face and a new band that her mother had bought for her the previous Christmas. "I'm going to be late for work," she thinks.

Faith has been working as a waitress at Bossier's Restaurant for the past six months. She would like to wear jeans to work, they're so much more comfortable than a skirt, but her boss, Eddie

Bossier, insists that his workers look nice. Faith grabs her purse, red with brown straps, and checks to make sure she has everything. Her apartment key, the key to her parents' apartment, her makeup bag, her glasses, her contact lens kit, some money and a paperback book. "Never know when I might have time to read," she thinks and smiles. Faith heads for the door. "I've got to go, Mom. I'm going to be late if I don't hurry."

Elizabeth Harvey stops Faith as she nears the door. "I'm glad you came by before you left for work," she says. Six months before, Faith had moved into an apartment in the same complex with another girl, and even though she lived less than two hundred feet away from her parents, Elizabeth Harvey still missed having her daughter at home with her and Vern.

"Do you really have to work tonight?" Elizabeth Harvey asks. She had already started missing her daughter, even though she wouldn't be leaving for New Orleans and the Army until tomorrow afternoon.

"I wasn't supposed to work tonight," Faith says. "But I said I'd fill in for one of the girls who has a test tomorrow. Besides, it's my last chance to be a waitress before I leave to see the world," she says and laughs.

As Faith turns to go, Elizabeth says, "Faith, wait. You've got a tear in your shoe. Go change them before you go."

Faith looks down at her sandals and sees that there is a small rip in the toe of the one on her right foot. "Mom, it's OK. There's really not time," she says. "I'm late. I'll see you later."

"How are you going to get to work?" Elizabeth Harvey asks.

"Rhoda said that she needs to go to the grocery store. She said that she would drive me over to Bossier's." Rhoda Cofield was a friend of Faith's who also lived in the Monroe Apartments.

And with that, Faith was gone out the door. Elizabeth Harvey would never see her daughter again.

Elizabeth Harvey settled down on the couch and turned on the television. Within a few minutes, the evening news came on. The lead stories were the presidential primaries for the 1980 presidential election. Primaries had been held that day in Arkansas, Nevada, Kentucky and Idaho. By evening, the winners of these primaries would be announced: President Jimmy Carter on the Democratic side and Ronald Reagan on the Republican side. Rescue operations continued on the site of the eruption of Mt. St. Helens near Vancouver, Washington. After eight months of captivity, the hostages were still being held in Iran. In Fort Chafee, Arkansas, a number of Cuban refugees had escaped the base. Criticizing the camp's security was then Governor Bill Clinton.

Bossier's Restaurant, Mandeville, Louisiana. 8:00 P.M., May 27, 1980. "I'll be over there in just a few minutes," Faith says. She picks up the receiver and dials her mother's number. After a few rings, her mother picks up. "Hello," she says.

"Hey, Mom. How's it going?" Faith says.

"Fine. You still at work?" Elizabeth Harvey asks.

"Yeah. I'm still at work. Listen, when I finish up here, I think I'll go out with some of my friends tonight. I won't be seeing them for a while, and so I thought I'd go to the Lakefront Disco after work. You don't mind, do you?" Faith asked.

Elizabeth had hoped to see Faith before she went to bed, but she understood Faith's desire to have a last night out with her high school friends. "It's fine. Just don't stay out too late."

"I won't," Faith says. "I'll come by in the morning, and we can finish up my packing, OK?"

"OK, dear," Elizabeth says.

"Good night, Mom."

"Good night, Faith. See you tomorrow."

When Elizabeth Harvey hung up the phone, there was no way for her to know that she would never hear Faith's voice again.

Faith replaced the phone on the cradle and went back to work. After her shift, she changed into a pair of jeans and a red-checked shirt that tied around the waist. She stayed at Bossier's for awhile and played pool with a couple of friends. After they left, she headed over to the Lakefront Disco.

When Faith walked into the Lakefront Disco, several of her friends greeted her. She had a few drinks and listened to music. She danced with some of the boys and chatted with some of the girls. She celebrated her last night of freedom from responsibility.

Faith was last seen alive at around 1:30 A.M. outside the Lakefront Disco, talking to two men. No one saw her leave. No one saw her get into a car or truck with anyone. Although no one will ever know for sure, it would appear that Faith simply decided to walk home at the end of the evening. It was a beautiful spring night. The lake was shimmering in the moonlight. This was her last night at home, the last night she would be able to walk the familiar streets and see the familiar sights. Perhaps she decided to stroll home and breathe in all the sensations of familiar places and things that made up the place she loved. And besides, it was a small town. Mandeville was not a dangerous place. It was a small town where everyone knew everyone else. What was the harm in walking home? It was only a few blocks from her apartment—surely no more than a fifteen-minute stroll in the cool breeze off the lake.

But she never made it.

How tantalizingly close to home Faith must have felt when the headlights of the truck washed over her, and she heard the cursing and felt the rough hands of strangers on her. Did she know then that her life was about to end or did she hold out hope for an escape?

As the truck sped away down Monroe Street carrying a terrified young girl and her laughing captors, did Faith look back over her shoulder and see a light on in her parents' apartment? Could she see her own apartment as she disappeared into the darkness of the night with the two men who now held her life in their hands?

LOSS OF FAITH

At 2:30 A.M., about an hour after Faith was last seen alive outside the Lakefront Disco talking with two men, Robert Willie banged on the door of the Chicken Town restaurant in Covington, a business that he had been convicted of burglarizing just a few years earlier.

"Let me in," he said in his slow, deep drawl.

"Who is it?" Jim Hano, the owner, said.

"It's Willie. Come on and unlock the door."

Hano thought about telling Willie to get lost, but he also knew that Willie was not a person to let small grievances go unpunished. At least he was knocking instead of breaking in. Hano decided to open the door.

Willie grinned at him. "Hey, Jim, how's it going? Give me three cups of ice, OK?"

After Hano gave Willie the ice, Willie left and Hano locked up, relieved that nothing had happened. Before he closed the door, Hano saw that Willie was in a pickup, but it was too dark to see who was with him in the truck.

Later, through the dirty, brown bandana covering her eyes, Faith Hathaway can see the sky beginning to lighten, her long night of terror finally becoming day. Robert Lee Willie, the smaller of the two strangers who had ripped her from a street near her home at knifepoint, sits against her, the touch of his jeans electric against her bare thigh. Faith tries to empty her

37

mind, just as she had done earlier during the rapes. As Joe Vaccaro, the larger of the two strangers, races through the fading darkness on the deserted Louisiana two-laner between Mandeville and Franklinton, Faith tries to focus on something—anything—beyond the confines of the truck where she is trapped with these two men. But all she can hear is the roar of the engine and all she can smell is the stench of sweat, beer, and the rough and unwanted sex the two strangers had forced on her.

Faith prays that the approaching dawn signals the end of the nightmare. Faith has told Willie and Vaccaro that she will not identify them. She has begged them not to hurt her, but they have just laughed. They are laughing now.

Later that day, deep in the piney woods, just a few miles outside of Franklinton, shafts of sunlight slice through the branches of trees, dappling the pinkish sandy floor of the deep, wooded gully known locally as Fricke's Cave. The air is still and hot. A tomb-like silence envelops the woods, broken only by the occasional whistling of a bird, the singsong chirping of tree frogs and crickets and the buzzing of flies.

The air is sweet and full of the bursting aroma of late spring in Fricke's Cave—wildflowers, damp and rotting logs, the smell of the nearby Bogue Chitto River carried effortlessly through the woods on drafts of occasional breezes.

This is a wild place, a beautiful place, where families come for picnics, and where the sounds of nature are often mixed with the sound of children's laughter. But today, something is wrong. There is a malevolent presence in Fricke's Cave. Evil has been here, in this place of beauty and light. In the midst of the teeming life of Fricke's Cave, there is death.

As breezes blow through Fricke's Cave and rustle the leaves of the trees overhead, as the birds hop about and sing their songs, as a mile away the Bogue Chitto River flows by with children swimming and laughing and old men fishing, here lost in the deep woods, down on the sandy floor of the cave lies the body of

Faith Colleen Hathaway. Her night of terror did not end with the dawn.

Faith is completely nude. Her arms are outstretched over her head, her legs are spread wide apart, her knees drawn up with her feet on the ground. Blood and gore cover her face, throat and chest. She has been stabbed seventeen times. Two of the fingers on her right hand are missing and lie nearby on the sandy floor of the cave. Already, insects are gathering, the smell of death and imminent decay a call to feast on this unexpected presence in their midst. Faith's face is turned to the side, and her mouth is wide-open. Her eyes too are open, frozen in a mask of pain and horror as her life ebbed away. Her face is bruised and bloody. Several of her teeth are missing, and most of them are loose from the battering she has suffered. Her inner thighs are scraped raw, and her vagina is torn and ravaged.

All of these wounds are now starting to attract the attention of the flies that buzz around her body. Soon they will begin to deposit their eggs in these bloody receptacles, and maggots will begin to multiply and commence the body's inevitable descent into decay and decomposition.

By late afternoon on May 28, Elizabeth has not heard from Faith. She checks with Faith's roommate and learns that Faith did not return home the night before. This is odd, but still it is possible that Faith has decided to spend the night with one of her girlfriends. But as the afternoon progresses and still no word comes from Faith, Elizabeth and Vernon Harvey's concern turns to panic.

Around 5:00 P.M., the Harveys call the Mandeville Police and report Faith missing. The police tell them that not enough time has passed to consider this a missing person case. Young people drop out of sight all the time, they say. After all, this is an eighteen-year-old girl. Maybe she has driven to Florida or Texas with some friends. Maybe she has changed her mind about leaving for the Army and has decided to simply vanish for awhile. Surely, the Harveys will hear from her. What could happen here in Mandeville?

But as time passes and the Harveys speak with friends of Faith's who know nothing of her whereabouts and who all say that they last saw here around 1:30, the Harveys' dread turns to a heart-chilling fear. Something has happened to their little girl, something terrible.

Slowly, the afternoon fades into night and still no word from Faith. Vernon goes out driving the streets of Mandeville, looking for any sign of his little girl. Stopping his car occasionally to yell out her name, he is a pathetic sight. People stop what they are doing and watch this man yelling out, "Faith, Faith."

Do they think he is a religious fanatic? Do they wonder who Faith is? Do they see him as a poor old father whose daughter has decided to run away? Is it possible that Faith's killers are nearby and are hearing these calls for help and laughing at the crazy old man?

Ironically, on May 28, 1980, the day that Faith is murdered, ABC's Nightline features a story on the imminent execution of a convicted murderer in the Georgia electric chair and the death penalty.

JOE VACCARO

———— ✨ ————

The Stardust Lounge, St. Tammany Parish, Louisiana. 10:30 P.M., Wednesday, May 28, 1980. About the time that Nightline is airing its story on Georgia's electric chair, St. Tammany Parish Deputy Sheriff Donald Sharp is at the Stardust Lounge, winding down after a long day. Although it is a popular nightspot in rural St. Tammany Parish, the Stardust Lounge is in reality merely a large, gray doublewide trailer that has been moved from Franklinton to the junction of U.S. 190 and Louisiana State Highway 25 and turned into a bar. The original owner, John Pierce, has named the bar after his favorite Las Vegas casino. A dark and gloomy pall seems to hang over the Stardust Lounge. It is a place for serious drinking.

Donald Sharp stands by the U-shaped bar near the front door, listening to the country music that booms from the jukebox located near the back wall. Among the men and women sitting at the eight or nine tables nearby, Donald notices a man that he knows from his days working as the jailer in the St. Tammany Parish jail—Joe Vaccaro.

Vaccaro is with a redhead whom Donald recognizes as a girl named Cindy. Sitting with Joe Vaccaro and Cindy at the table is a man in his early twenties drinking a bottle of beer and smoking a cigarette.

Donald takes his glass with him and walks over to the table where Vaccaro, Cindy and the other man are sitting. "Mind if I join you?" he asks.

41

Vaccaro stares silently at Donald for a moment as if considering his options. He pushes his chair back and stands in front of Donald. "Hey, man," he says. "Walk over to the bar with me and buy me a beer."

Donald nods at Cindy and the stranger, and then follows Vaccaro to the bar. "What's up, Joe?" he says.

Vaccaro glances around the bar as if he is looking for someone. "Listen, I can't talk here, but I've got something I need to talk to you about. Something real important."

"What is it?" Donald asks.

Vaccaro shakes his head. "Not here. I'll call you tomorrow. I've got to go now. We'll talk tomorrow."

As Vaccaro quickly walks back to the table, Donald stands at the bar, puzzling over Vaccaro's strange behavior.

The next day, Donald Sharp drives from Covington to New Orleans on official business. When he returns home that evening, he stops by his mother's house.

"Some boy named Joe's been calling here all day," Donald's mother tells him. "He won't say what he wants. Just says that he wants to talk to you."

When Donald arrives at home, his wife says the same thing—a boy named Joe has called three or four times during the day, extremely anxious to speak with him.

Although it is past 9:00 P.M., Donald decides to call Joe Vaccaro. Maybe he has some information on a case. Since he knows that Vaccaro has been staying with his grandmother, he tries her number first.

"Joe's not here," she tells him. "I'll have him call you, though, Deputy Sharp." When Donald finally goes to bed a couple of hours later, Vaccaro has not called back.

The next evening, Friday, May 30, at about 7:00 P.M., the phone rings at Donald's house. "Hello?" he says. In the background, he can hear music and loud talking, the sounds of a barroom.

"Hey, Deputy Sharp, it's me, Joe Vaccaro."

"What's going on, Joe?" he asks. "What's so important that you want to talk to me about?"

"Listen, I'm back at the Stardust Lounge," Vaccaro says. "I'm here with Robert Willie." After a pause, Vaccaro says almost in a whisper, "I need to talk to you, man, but I can't talk on the phone about this."

Donald glances at his watch. He had been looking forward to a nice, quiet Friday evening at home. Still, he knows that it may be important. "I can come down to the Sheriff's Office in Covington and meet you in the alley between the courthouse and the tavern," Donald says.

"No," Vaccaro says. "I've got to get away from Willie first."

"What's going on, Joe?" Donald asks.

"I can't talk now. I'll call you back around nine-thirty, and we can meet somewhere. Not at the Sheriff's Office, though. I'm too messed up."

"OK, listen, I'll be here. Call back later," Donald says.

"Yeah, I will," Vaccaro says and then hangs up. Although Donald waits, Vaccaro never calls back.

A few hours later, in Mandeville, Louisiana. A young woman walks briskly out of the front door of a Chinese restaurant on U.S. 190 near the approach to the Lake Pontchartrain causeway. She stretches and rubs her sore neck. "What a day," she says. She has just finished her shift as a waitress, and she is still dressed in her uniform. As she walks toward her car, she visualizes her nice warm bed at home.

Suddenly, her reverie is broken as a beat-up pickup truck quickly swings over toward her. In that moment, she can see that there are two filthy-looking men in the truck. Her eyes meet those of the skinny, blonde-haired man hanging out the passenger-side window, and she senses that she is in real danger. As the reflection from the restaurant's neon sign spills over the truck, she sees what looks like the glint of a gun barrel.

She runs for her car while, behind her, she can hear the truck's tires as it screeches from the parking lot and out onto the highway. She jumps into her car and quickly locks the doors. For several moments, all she can do is grip the steering wheel as her heart races and blood pounds in her ears.

Later that same night. It is midnight, a few miles away in the quaint village of Madisonville, Louisiana. A young couple sits in a car parked on the riverfront. The windows are rolled down so that they can feel the warm breeze off Lake Pontchartrain as they watch the moon's reflection softly undulating on the dark surface of the Tchefuncte River. They too are about to come face to face with evil—the same evil that ripped the life from Faith Hathaway, whose body still lies undiscovered in Fricke's Cave.

THE TERROR CONTINUES

Madisonville, Louisiana. 12:05 A.M., Saturday, May 31, 1980.
Madisonville is a small town unaccustomed to violence. Large, stately homes line the Tchefuncte River that flows through town and empties into Lake Pontchartrain. The bridge over the river—an old metal drawbridge—is reminiscent of a simpler, more innocent time. The riverfront is bordered by a row of trees that line a narrow, grassy area between the river and parking for several small shops and restaurants. It is an area that is treasured by the citizens of Madisonville, many of whom regularly spend time sitting in their cars or lounging on the banks of the river.

No more than a few hundred feet from the riverfront is Badeaux's, a quintessential, small-town, drive-in restaurant. It is here on this night that sixteen-year-old Debbie Lynn Cuevas and her twenty-year-old boyfriend, Mark Brewster, have stopped for milkshakes after going to a movie in nearby Covington. Debbie and Mark get back into Mark's car, a black 1978 Thunderbird with red pin stripes, a red interior and T-tops, and, in just a few seconds, Mark pulls the Thunderbird into a spot beneath a towering live oak tree on the riverfront. He cuts the engine, and he and Debbie sit and talk and drink their milkshakes.

Debbie is pretty and very petite, just five feet three inches and one hundred six pounds. It is a beautiful, balmy night, and she is dressed casually, wearing a brown camisole top and blue jeans. They roll their windows down, letting the perfumed night air flow into the car.

As they sit in Mark's Thunderbird, a blue 1962 Ford pickup truck pulls up on the other side of one of the many live oak trees lining the riverfront. A few minutes later, the truck pulls out and then parks next to Mark's car.

Mark and Debbie can see that the men in the truck look wild, their hair long and greasy. Mark begins to roll up his window, but as he does, the men in the truck jump out and run over to the Thunderbird. One of them, a skinny blonde-haired man, shoves a sawed-off, break-down, twelve-gauge shotgun in the window. The other man, only slightly larger, brandishes a .22 caliber five-shot, nickel-plated revolver. The men throw the car doors open and jump into the Thunderbird. The smaller man gets in the back seat. The other pushes Mark aside and takes the wheel.

The car is immediately filled with an overpowering stench. Both of the men are filthy, their breath a sickening mixture of booze and cigarettes. They are not much older than Debbie and Mark, perhaps in their early twenties. The taller of the two, the one with the revolver, is only about five feet eight inches tall and one hundred forty pounds. He has green eyes, brown hair and a moustache. He is wearing blue jeans and a long-sleeve black shirt with a red stripe across the front and a star in the center.

The other man, barely five feet six or seven inches tall and only one hundred twenty-five pounds, has long blonde hair and blue eyes. He is wearing a black cap, a tan and blue shirt, white jeans, and brown boots. On the upper part of his right arm is a tattoo of a cross and the name "Peggy." On his left forearm is a tattoo of the name "Pam."

The shorter man appears to be the leader. "We're escapees from Angola," he says. "We've killed before, and we'll kill again if you don't do what we say." He stares at Debbie before continuing. "We only want the car," he says. "We'll drop you two off down the road a piece."

The Thunderbird disappears in a rush down the road while the old truck sits empty on the banks of the Tchefuncte River. Three days after the disappearance of Faith Hathaway in Mandeville, two more young people, this time a sixteen-year-old girl and her twenty-year-old boyfriend, have disappeared. The innocence of the rural Northshore area has been shattered forever.

DEBBIE AND MARK

Madisonville, Louisiana. 8:00 A.M., Sunday, June 1, 1980. As sea birds bank and glide over Lake Pontchartrain in the early morning hours of Sunday, June 1, an old, grayish-brown Chrysler New Yorker with orange racing stripes down the sides slows down on the highway just inside Madisonville, and a young girl is pushed out of the car. As the car speeds away into the distance, the sobbing girl begins to run down the highway.

Debbie bursts into her uncle's grocery store, her eyes full of terror, still fearful that the two men who had kidnapped her and Mark would be coming back for her. Finally, her uncle succeeds in calming her down, and the police are called. Debbie identifies her kidnappers as Robert Lee Willie and Joe Vaccaro. The story that sixteen-year-old Debbie Cuevas tells is bone-chilling.

After Willie and Vaccaro forced their way into Mark's car, Vaccaro slid into the driver's seat next to Mark. He held a .22 caliber revolver in his right hand as he drove with his left. Willie climbed into the back seat of the car and held a sawed-off shotgun close to their heads.

After a few miles, Vaccaro stopped the car and forced Mark into the trunk. At this point, Willie made Debbie get in the back seat of the Thunderbird with him. Now alone in the front seat, Vaccaro turned onto Louisiana Highway 1077, and they rocketed down the road.

Debbie hunched up in the corner of the back seat as far away from Willie as she could. "Take off your clothes," Willie said.

She told him no and began to cry. "Please just leave me alone," she begged.

Vaccaro stuck the pistol over the back of the seat at Debbie. Willie placed the shotgun on the floorboard of the back seat and pulled off his shirt and boots.

"You better take off your clothes and do what I say," Willie said. When Debbie refused, Willie began pulling her clothes off. He then pulled off his pants and pushed her down on the seat. Debbie turned her head away as Willie tried to kiss her.

"You had better like it," he said. As Vaccaro drove Mark's Thunderbird down the nearly deserted country roads of rural St. Tammany Parish, Willie raped Debbie. Afterwards, Debbie cleaned herself with a dirty, brown bandana that she found lying on the floor of the car—the same bandana that Willie and Vaccaro had used to blindfold Faith as they led her down the hill at Fricke's Cave.

When they reached the junction with Interstate 10, Vaccaro pulled onto it and headed east. After a while, Vaccaro stopped the car and Willie pulled Mark out of the trunk and pushed him into the backseat with Debbie. Willie climbed into the front seat next to Vaccaro. They drove on in the early morning darkness. Near Ocean Springs, Mississippi, Vaccaro stopped once again, and Willie once again forced Mark back into the trunk.

As they neared Pascagoula, Mississippi, Willie pulled some pills from his pocket. He handed a couple to Vaccaro and kept a couple for himself.

"What's that?" Debbie asked.

Willie grinned. "This here's a black Molly," he said. "And this one's a yellow Molly. Speed, Blondie, speed."

After he swallowed the pills, Willie stared at Debbie for a long time. "How old are you?" he asked.

She told him that she was sixteen.

"I'm twenty-two," he said. He took out his wallet, removed a piece of paper from it and handed it to Debbie.

"This here's my probation discharge letter," he said. "It's got my birthday on it, January 2, 1958." Debbie also saw his name at the top of the paper: Robert Lee Willie.

As they approached Mobile, Alabama, Mark began to beat on the trunk and scream that he could not breathe. Vaccaro pulled the car off the road at the Wilcox Road exit.

Willie opened the trunk and pulled Mark out. "Come on," he said and pushed Mark roughly down a narrow dirt road there that led into some woods. A few minutes later, Willie returned alone.

Willie glanced briefly at Debbie, before turning to Vaccaro. "Come on, Joe. I want to show you where I left him," he said. "Let's put her in the trunk first." They placed Debbie in the trunk of the car and headed back into the woods.

After a moment, Debbie pushed hard against the lid of the trunk, but it was shut tight. There was nothing to do but wait. She was trapped. At that moment, Debbie heard the sound of people struggling in the woods. Then, she heard the distinct popping sound of a pistol being fired. A second shot followed immediately.

A minute or so later, the trunk lid opened. "Get out," Willie said. He dragged her out and put her back in the car.

As Vaccaro pulled back onto the road and headed for the interstate, Debbie said, "What were those shots?"

"Oh, just some hunters," Willie said.

"I know what a rifle sounds like," Debbie said. "That was not a rifle."

Willie grinned. "We were just trying to scare that boyfriend of yours," Willie said. "We shot up into the air, and he went running into the woods."

After heading east towards Florida for a few minutes, Willie decided that they should head back to Louisiana. Vaccaro turned the car around in the median, and they headed back home.

During the afternoon as they drove seemingly without purpose through Washington and St. Tammany Parishes, Vaccaro looked over at Debbie and said, "You sure are nicer than our last girlfriend." Vaccaro told her that he hoped the same thing that had happened to that girlfriend did not happen to her. When Debbie asked what had happened, Vaccaro said, "Oh, it was terrible. Things got out of control, and she got raped and her throat cut from ear to ear."

Saturday afternoon, May 31. Near Franklinton, Louisiana. Debbie had now been held captive for more than twelve hours. Vaccaro pulled the Thunderbird onto a gravel road that led to a dirt road and which made a dead end at the top of a large gorge.

"We've got to stretch our legs and think things over," Willie said. He and Vaccaro walked behind the car and talked where she could not hear them. After a few minutes, Vaccaro walked away from the car, climbed a fence and headed into the woods.

Willie came back to the car. "Why don't you just take me home?" Debbie asked him.

"I'm going to take you home after I make love to you, Blondie," he said.

"No, I won't do it. You might as well go ahead and kill me now," Debbie said.

"Blondie, nobody's going to kill you," he said. He pointed the shotgun at Debbie and told her to take her clothes off.

Debbie began to cry, but she did as she was told. Willie pushed her down on the front seat of the car and raped her for the second time. After it was over, Willie said, "You are finished, Blondie. Get up and get dressed."

A few minutes later, Vaccaro came back from the woods and got back in the car with Willie and Debbie. He pulled the car back onto the road, and they continued their aimless driving.

At around 5:00 P.M., Willie and Vaccaro ran into a friend of theirs, Tommy Holden, driving an old, grayish-brown Chrysler New Yorker. He was in his late twenties, had long brown hair and a beard, and was bigger than Willie or Vaccaro, about five feet eleven inches tall and one hundred seventy-five pounds. Willie told him that Debbie was a friend of theirs, and that the Thunderbird belonged to her. He told Holden to follow them to River Road. When they got there, they pulled both cars off the main road and into a wooded area near the power lines. Then, Willie, Vaccaro and Debbie all got into the New Yorker with Holden.

They continued to ride around. Around 8:00 P.M., they stopped at Holden's trailer. As they pulled up in the yard, Holden's Siberian husky puppy, Missy, ran up to greet him.

After they had been in the trailer for a while, Vaccaro came up to Debbie. "Listen," he said. "Willie is mad 'cause he's the only one who's had sex with you. He wants me to do it, too."

Vaccaro took Debbie into the front bedroom of the trailer. "The only reason I'm doing this is because Willie won't take you home until I do," he said. The room was in near darkness. "Take off your clothes," Vaccaro said. "Let's get it over with. I've got to leave the door open, though," Vaccaro said. "Robert wants to make sure we're really doing it."

Debbie pleaded with Vaccaro not to do this, but Vaccaro said he had to do it. He began to kiss her. Debbie turned her head to avoid him, but it was no use. Vaccaro raped her. When it was over, they returned to the living room where Willie and Holden were watching television.

Since it was now late, Willie and Vaccaro and Holden, tired and more than a little drunk from all the beer and pills, decided to call it a night. Debbie was lying on the couch. "Get off," Willie told her harshly. "You can sleep on the floor."

Willie made a makeshift leash by tying a rope around Debbie's wrists and tying the end of the rope to his own arm. If she tried to get away, Willie would know it.

As Debbie lay on the floor, exhaustion overcame her, and she fell asleep. At some point during the night, though, she woke up and discovered Holden rubbing his hands over her body. She began to scream, pushing his hands away.

"Behave now," he said.

"Don't touch me," Debbie said. "I'm tired of this."

"Well, here I have been so nice to you, letting you stay at my house and all, and you're not even going to show your thanks," he said.

"Y'all are planning on killing me," Debbie said. "I know it. I'm not going to stand for this anymore. If y'all are going to hurt me, y'all are just going to have to hurt me. That's it. I'm not going through this again."

Holden looked confused at Debbie's words.

"Y'all can shoot me and take me down the road and dump me, but I'm not going through this again," she said. Holden got up from the floor angry and apparently still unaware that Debbie had been kidnapped.

The next morning, they all got back in Holden's New Yorker and drove back to the power lines near River Road where Mark's Thunderbird was hidden. Willie and Vaccaro began talking about what to do.

Willie wanted to kill Debbie, just put her in the car and set it on fire. Holden heard this and was incredulous. "I won't have any part of killing her," he said. "I won't let you kill her. If you try to kill her, you'll have to kill me first."

Willie became irate at Holden, but he backed down. "All right, all right," he said. "We'll take her home."

They piled back into Holden's car and drove back towards Madisonville. It was now around 8:00 A.M. As families throughout Madisonville woke on this Sunday morning and began to prepare for church, Tommy Holden's New Yorker slowed and then stopped not far from where Mark and Debbie had been kidnapped more than thirty hours earlier. The door opened. "Get out," Willie said.

Debbie stumbled out of the car, her first moment of freedom since just after midnight on Saturday morning. At first, Debbie walked slowly down the road. The car pulled away, and when it was out of sight, she began to run. She ran up to the highway and into her uncle's grocery store.

Later that morning, a team of FBI agents converged on the field near Mobile, Alabama, where Willie and Vaccaro had taken Mark and where Debbie had heard the two gunshots. They found Mark in a sitting position tied to a tree. His hands had been tied together tightly with a shoelace and a belt, and then tied to one of the tree limbs. His tee shirt had been stuffed in his mouth as a gag. Mark had been stabbed in the side and his throat had been cut. He also had been shot twice in the back of the head at point-blank range. He was covered in blood. But he was alive.

When the FBI found Mark, he was only able to open one of his eyes. He was unable to speak, and he was terrified when the FBI rescue team first approached him. He only calmed down when he realized that the men in the rescue party meant him no harm.

Just as it was miraculous that Debbie had lived to tell her story, so God smiled on Mark that day. Although his injuries were extreme and life-threatening, Mark Brewster had survived a monstrous attempt to kill him.

FRICKE'S CAVE

Fricke's Cave, south of Franklinton, Louisiana. Sunday afternoon, June 1, 1980. Just a few hours after Debbie Cuevas burst into her uncle's grocery store in nearby Madisonville, a family from the Franklinton area did what many others did on a Sunday afternoon in rural Washington Parish—they went to Fricke's Cave for a picnic.

Fricke's Cave is not a cave in the usual sense of the word. Rather, it is a beautiful wilderness area located in a gorge near the Bogue Chitto River just a few miles outside of Franklinton. In order to enter the Cave, you must walk sideways, sliding and hanging on to the limbs of trees or small bushes as you descend the seventy-five feet or so of the bluff into the Cave. It's a steep walk down the bluff, probably close to a forty-five degree angle.

Once in the Cave, you find yourself in a natural wonderland. Streams flow through the Cave and the whole area is wooded and alive with trees, bushes, wildflowers and small animal life. It is quite lovely, but dense and hot in the summer. Tall trees tower over the area and, in the depths of the woods, the sun's rays barely penetrate the canopy of trees that flourish overhead. The floor of the Cave is sandy, and it is a beautiful pinkish color. On many of the walls of the bluff, the sand has been formed over time into intricate, conical shapes resembling stalagmites.

When I was a boy, and even up until the terrible crime spree of 1980, schools would have whole classes of small children, preschoolers and older, come to Fricke's Cave for field trips. It was a treasure for our small town of Franklinton. Just a few weeks before the disappearance of Faith Hathaway in Mandeville, the state of Louisiana purchased Fricke's Cave, planning to turn it into a state preservation area. Now, more than twenty years later, the state still owns Fricke's Cave, but it is barren of people, no longer the oasis it once was. Today, there is a locked gate across the road near the highway that leads to Fricke's Cave.

On Sunday, June 1, 1980, however, Fricke's Cave was still a popular place for families to gather, and it was a beautiful day for a picnic on that Sunday afternoon long ago. The picnickers were perhaps unaware of the disappearance of Faith Hathaway in Mandeville on the previous Wednesday. After all, Mandeville was another town in another parish, closer to New Orleans and far away from the rural simplicity of Washington Parish. And besides, this was Fricke's Cave, a place of safety, beauty and refuge that countless generations of young people from the area had grown up playing in. They were also probably unaware of the disappearance of Mark Brewster and Debbie Cuevas from Madisonville. Even if they knew, this too was far removed from Fricke's Cave.

So just a few hours after Debbie Cuevas came running and stumbling into her uncle's grocery store in Madisonville, a group of family and friends made their way into Fricke's Cave, a picnic lunch in hand.

Picture this, a group of small children, laughing and running through the dense trees of the Cave, young people walking alone in the beauty of the cave, perhaps holding hands and whispering to each other, lunch laid out.

There were about a dozen members in the group of family and friends out for a lazy day in Fricke's Cave. Among them were Tracey Barber and a friend of his, Lynette McElveen. Also, in the group were several members of Tracey's family—his mother, his father, his sisters and two of his nephews. There were also several family friends.

Tracey was walking around with Lynette and with the smaller

children when his little sister stumbled over a purse and some clothing lying on the sandy floor of

Fricke's Cave. It looked as if there had been a scuffle here. There were footprints in the sand and papers were scattered and a blouse and skirt were wadded up and hanging out of the purse. A makeup case, a contact lens kit and lots of papers were also inside the purse. Lying nearby in the open was a pair of panties.

Tracey picked up the purse and the other things and took them back to show to his group. When they had finished their picnic, they took the purse and the belongings to the Sheriff's Office in Franklinton.

Deputy L. M. James was working on that Sunday afternoon in Franklinton at the Sheriff's Office as a radio operator. He looked through the purse and found Faith Hathaway's drivers license. He looked through the things and found a phone number and dialed it, but no one answered. He next placed a call to the St. Tammany Sheriff's Office and asked if there was a missing person by the name of Faith Hathaway. Of course, the answer was yes.

THE INVESTIGATION BEGINS

On the day after Faith's purse was found in Fricke's Cave, I was sitting at my desk in the District Attorney's AOffice where I had been working as chief investigator for District Attorney Marion "KO" Farmer since I had left the Washington Parish Sheriff's Office about eighteen months earlier. I was unaware that I was about to receive a call that would mark a turning point in my life.

Looking back on my days of relative innocence before I received that call, I can clearly remember the precise moment that I decided I wanted to be a criminal investigator and, more particularly, a homicide detective. I was still a uniformed deputy at the time. I had asked Sheriff Willie Jay Blair to place me in charge of a jury in a first-degree murder trial of a man charged with shooting his victim in the back and then robbing him.

During the trial, I hung on every word from Judge Hillary Crain and from the lawyers and the witnesses. When the jury returned from its deliberations, the courtroom was electric with tension and excitement. I watched closely as Judge Crain ordered the clerk of court to read and record the verdict. Guilty. A short time later, the jury retired to decide whether the defendant should be sentenced to life in prison or to death.

A few hours later, I was told that the jury had reached a verdict. As I escorted the jury members back into the courtroom, I was certain that the sentence would be death. I was wrong.

The clerk read the jury's verdict of life in prison. As I watched the reaction of the victim's family, I could easily tell how disappointed they were in the verdict. From what I had overheard during deliberations while I stood watch just outside the door to the jury room, I felt certain that the defendant would be sentenced to death. Still, it was obvious to me that although the detectives had worked hard and long on the case, the jury was not satisfied that they had completely uncovered the truth. Even though I think the jurors all believed that the defendant deserved a sentence of death, they had not reached that point of moral certainty they needed—they had not been presented with all the facts necessary to return a death sentence.

I was worthless as a jailer after that trial. Everything that had been exciting to me before was no longer of interest to me. I had changed drastically overnight. I was determined to become a thorn in the side of Duane Blair, the sheriff's son and my friend, on a daily basis in order to get him to recommend to his father to send to me to the police academy. And aggravate him, I did.

A couple of weeks after the murder trial, having worried the sheriff and his son into submission, I was allowed to enter the police academy. I worked hard and graduated at the top of the class. Then, after more browbeating, Sheriff Blair agreed to let me become a detective. Less than a year after first being sworn in as a uniformed deputy sheriff, I had reached detective status.

Now, eighteen months after having left my job as a detective for the Sheriff's Office to work as the chief investigator for the District Attorney's Office, I received the call that would change the course of my life.

Peggy Jones, my secretary, walked into my office. "Mike, Richard Newman is on the line for you," she said. Richard had moved into my spot at the Sheriff's Office when I left to work for the District Attorney.

"Hey, Richard, what's going on?" I asked.

"Mike, some picnickers at Fricke's Cave found a girl's clothing and a purse containing a wallet and other personal items," Richard said. "The girl is a missing person from Mandeville."

"What's her name?" I asked.

It was a name that has changed the course of my life. "Faith Hathaway," Richard said.

FAITH IS FOUND

On Sunday evening after Faith's belongings were discovered at Fricke's Cave, Richard Newman and a couple of other deputies went with Tracey Barber back to Fricke's Cave and searched for about an hour until it became too dark to continue that evening. The next day, however, word got out, and almost immediately Fricke's Cave became a zoo. Local law enforcement agents, the media, everyone converged on Fricke's Cave. In addition, since Debbie Cuevas had been raped at a place matching the description of Fricke's Cave, FBI agents investigating the crimes committed against Mark and Debbie also searched the Cave.

Unfortunately, the two persons who had the greatest right to know about the discovery of Faith's belongings—Vern and Elizabeth Harvey—were not notified. I sincerely regret that the first thing I did on Monday when Richard Newman called me was not to call the Harveys. Somehow the Harveys found out, though, and they were soon there searching for Faith.

For two full days, Monday and Tuesday, June 2 and 3, the FBI, the St. Tammany Parish Sheriff's Office, the Mandeville Police, the Washington Parish Sheriff's Office, Faith's family, and volunteers combed the area. Several hundred people searched the Cave. Someone in Faith's family, one of her cousins, I believe, even called in a psychic by the name of B.J. Commander. Finally, late on Tuesday, June 3, after Faith had been missing for almost a week, the search was called off. Everyone was convinced she was not in Fricke's Cave. Everyone except for me.

I did not believe that whoever had kidnapped Faith and had taken her down into the Cave had allowed her to leave there alive. As much as I hated to think about it, I knew in my heart that Faith was dead, and that her body had to be somewhere in Fricke's Cave. I even got into an argument with another deputy about giving up the search. "If you're so smart, why don't you find her?" he said.

Late on Tuesday, right after sundown, as darkness began to envelope Fricke's Cave, I went back to Fricke's Cave alone. I slid down the embankment of the Cave and began slowly walking through the woods. It was very quiet and still. Other than my feet thrashing through the dense undergrowth and the pounding of my heart, the only sounds were the crickets beginning to chirp as dusk turned to night.

I admit that I was frightened as I walked alone through the gloomy near-darkness of Fricke's Cave. I even got chills on the back of my neck. It is hard to explain, but I had the very real sense that something was askew here, that a place I had loved since I was a child had somehow changed forever, tainted by an unknown force of evil. I did not want to admit in court that I was scared as I searched for some trace of Faith that Tuesday evening in Fricke's Cave. I was young and brave then. I was not about to tell anybody I was scared. It's funny how twenty years can change your thinking. I have no problem admitting now to just how scared I really was.

I found nothing that first night. The next day I went to get my dad and his dog to help me search. Dad was not home, so I asked a friend of mine, an auxiliary deputy named Brian Lynch, to come with me.

It was brutally hot as Brian and I slipped and slid down into the Cave. That summer was the hottest one in Louisiana since 1896, when records were first kept. It was also the second driest. The weather had been scorching all week with no rain in sight. That day, the humidity was in the nineties and the temperature soared to ninety-five degrees. Down in the Cave, it was suffocating and my sweat-soaked shirt stuck to my skin. The air was still and close. No breeze and a lot of bugs. It was miserable.

As I walked through the underbrush of the Cave, swatting at mosquitoes and flies, the only sound was my own heavy breathing and the thumping of blood in my ears. After more than a quarter of an hour of tramping through the Cave and wondering if everyone else was right—that Faith was not here—I caught the first hint of an odor that I knew immediately was out of place here in Fricke's Cave, a faint, sickly sweet odor. I followed the odor, and it grew stronger and stronger as I walked. Finally, when the smell was nearly overpowering, I saw it.

I say "it" and not "her" because what I saw was no longer Faith Hathaway. It was the horrid, decomposing remains of what was left of Faith's body. It was only about one hundred fifty yards away from where Faith's purse and other belongings had been found.

I stood there in shock, my brain struggling to process just what I was seeing. There was a dull pounding in my head, and my ears were roaring like a train. I felt hot, and I thought I was going to faint. Instead, I threw up in my mouth, and then swallowed it back down. I hit one knee and gasped for air.

Faith's body was horribly bloated, and it was a dark, orange-brown color, almost like dried meat or tanned leather. A solid white line surrounded her body, as if a crime scene chalk-line had been drawn around her. This was surely a crime scene, but this was no ordinary chalk-line. It was a solid line of writhing maggots. The flesh of Faith's face was gone. Her head was skeletal and a dark, grayish black. There were gaping holes where Faith's eyes once had been. Her mouth was wide open as if Faith had died screaming. Her arms were stretched backwards over her head and her legs were spread as far apart as humanly possible.

There were large, white patches on Faith's neck and chest and in her vaginal area. At first, it looked like mold, but as I looked closer I saw that the white patches were undulating with life. In death, Faith's body was alive with a massive infestation of maggots.

Her throat appeared as though it had been ripped out, and her chest was full of stab wounds. Her right hand and fingers had been sliced to ribbons. Faith's Mexican-style sandals were lying by her right foot. Some of the skin of her left foot was detached and lying beside it. I remember noticing that the detached skin had a toenail on it. On her left arm was a watch, and there was a ring on one of the fingers of her left hand.

Time seems to stand still at a terrible moment such as this. Your senses become supercharged and extremely focused. Later, you remember the strangest details. For example, I remember noticing that Faith's fingernails were painted.

Although the sight of Faith's ravaged body almost defies description, the smell was worse. My God, the smell! The smell of a dead human body is totally different from that of a rotting animal. I don't know if it is psychological or not, but I know that it is different. It is sickeningly sweet, almost like sweet feces. It is ten times stronger than the smell of a dead animal.

As I stared at Faith's body, it seemed to me that what had once been a living body was now literally melting away. The appearance of what remained was of something wet and shiny. Bodily fluids were draining from Faith's decomposing body, killing the plant life around her.

It took several minutes for me to calm down and to start acting like a law officer. I called for Brian Lynch to go to the car and to radio Deputy Richard Newman and tell him to get the LSP Crime Lab to come immediately. Brian came by first to take a look. He threw up. Then, he started running. He told me later he ran all the way back to the top of Fricke's Cave. He never came back down.

As deputies started arriving at the scene, I asked one of them to go back to the entrance to Fricke's Cave off the highway and to set up a roadblock. No one was to enter unless I authorized it. The deputy in charge of the roadblock later told me that it had been the toughest job he had ever been assigned in all his years. He said that he started receiving threats about losing his job just several minutes after setting up the roadblock. He said he received so many threats that he started making a line in the dirt every time someone told him to let him in or they were going to "have his badge." At the end of the day there were scores of marks in the dirt. Cars were backed up all the way from Fricke's Cave to the highway. Newspaper and television reporters, family members, law enforcement officials and sightseers swarmed the main entrance.

After Charlie Andrews of the LSP crime lab had photographed Faith's body and collected samples of the maggots, District Attorney Marion Farmer and Assistant District Attorney Bill Alford came down into the Cave and viewed Faith's body.

Afterwards, when we were loading Faith's body into the body bag, I was up by her head, between her outstretched arms. When we picked her body up, Faith's head became almost totally detached from her body and landed on my boots. Bill threw up. Everybody screamed. I jumped back and dropped her. I gagged and gagged.

When I took the Harveys back to where I had found the body, I found the exact location because we had all left our plastic gloves there in a pile. I picked them up on the way out and threw them in an old box, which I put in the trunk of my car. I had to roll the windows down before I got back to Franklinton. I took the car by the Sheriff's Office and made the jail trustees clean out my trunk. I had to leave it overnight with the trunk open. It never smelled right again, always a little musky after that. It took four vodka and sodas and two pain killers for me to get to sleep that night.

I burned the clothes I was wearing when I found Faith's body, because no matter how many times I washed them they still smelled like death. Also, I burned my boots. I had to throw away the floor mats from my car. When I got home after the search, I smelled death on my skin.

After I found Faith's body, I began to take baths all night long. I would lie down and start dreaming, and I would wake up and smell the "smell" and go jump in the tub. I even pulled all the nose hairs out of my nose trying to make the smell go away. I can smell it as I write these words.

I remember having bad dreams for months after I found Faith's body. During this time, I avoided sleep because I did not want to dream. In my dreams, sometimes it would be my mother who was murdered and sometimes it would be my daughter, Jade. Even now, Faith occasionally comes to me in my sleep. She is alive, but her body is decomposed. I tell her that we thought she had died, and that we needed to get her back to her mother as soon as we can because she is worried sick. Faith just smiles. I have never been able to get her all the way back to Mandeville in my dreams.

After I found Faith's body, I began drinking heavily to dull my senses. I would drink myself to sleep every night. I would sleep for two or three hours, and then I would be wide-awake. Later, after the trials of Faith's killers, I quit going to the office. I had once loved my job. Now I hated it. I would use every excuse in the world not to show up at the office. Often I would just drive around and around the courthouse and then go back home. I was always filled with a terrible dread. I drank most of the day and all of the night.

CONFESSIONS OF MURDER

Less than twenty-four hours before I found Faith Hathaway's ravaged and decomposing body in the sweltering heat of Fricke's Cave, five hundred miles north of Franklinton, Robert Lee Willie and Joe Vaccaro, wanted for their crimes against Mark Brewster and Debbie Cuevas, were arrested along with Tommy Holden at the bus station in Hope, Arkansas, the birthplace of former President Bill Clinton.

Within a few days, both Willie and Vaccaro confessed to the kidnapping, rape and attempted murder involving Mark and Debbie. There was little else they could do. With Debbie's ability to testify and with Mark still alive, although not yet able to speak, there was little doubt that they would be convicted of these crimes.

Still, the big question for me as the lead investigator in Faith Hathaway's murder was whether Willie and Vaccaro were guilty of killing her. We had very little evidence tying Willie and Vaccaro to Faith's murder. I knew that even if they were guilty of killing Faith, and I believed that they were, it would be next to impossible to prove their guilt to a jury beyond a reasonable doubt unless they provided statements implicating themselves. Indeed, without a statement from them, it was unlikely that the district attorney would even be able to obtain an indictment in the case.

It was with this background that Sheriff Willie Jay Blair dispatched me to Arkansas to interview Willie and Vaccaro. "The governor's helicopter will be here to pick up you in an hour," Willie Jay said. "Take whoever you want and go talk to them boys."

I decided to take Deputy Donald Sharp because he knew Joe Vaccaro, and I thought Vaccaro might be willing to cooperate with Donald. I also asked Ronnie Pierce, a Louisiana State Police detective, to accompany us.

Our pilot was Louisiana State Policeman Walter Smith, the governor's main pilot. He landed the helicopter in the playground in front of the elementary school I had attended as a child. We took off and flew right over the high school from which I had graduated. We were flying very low, and I could see the roof of the school very clearly. I thought about how long it had been since I had been in high school, and about Faith Hathaway who had been murdered just a week after her high school graduation. My eyes began to fill with tears. I did not want the others to think I was weak, so I pretended that I had a cold.

While we flew the five hundred miles from Franklinton to Arkansas, I mentally rehearsed what I was going to do when we got there. My heart was racing as we piled into a car in Texarkana, which the FBI had waiting to take us to the jail.

As we drove to the jail, I checked over what we knew so far in our investigation into the murder of Faith Hathaway. In reality, it was not much. Based on the life cycle of the maggots found on Faith's body, we knew that she had died not long after she had last been seen alive at the Lakefront Disco. We knew that Faith had died as a result of her stab wounds, but the murder weapon was not found at the scene. We had reason to suspect Willie and Vaccaro, particularly after they released Debbie, and she related her story. Still, we had no direct evidence. The District Attorney's Office was in a state of despair. Without a confession, things were not looking good.

When I arrived at the jail, I decided to interview Joe Vaccaro first. From what I had been told, he would likely be more willing to talk than Willie. When Vaccaro was brought into the interview room, he was still dressed in his street clothes and not in jail garb. The first thing I did was to allow him to have the handcuffs removed. I wanted him to trust me, to think of me as someone who was on his side. The FBI had already played the bad cops with Willie and him. I was going to play the good cop.

My first attempt to question Vaccaro was a failure. He wouldn't tell me anything. In addition, he said that Willie would have nothing to say to me either. Vaccaro almost had me convinced that my coming to Arkansas was a big waste of time. Still, I figured that since I had come all the way up here, I was at least going to get a look at the infamous Robert Lee Willie.

My first impression of Robert Lee Willie was that he was a cocky young punk, trying to play bad. He walked with a swagger in his step, be-bopping and bouncing on the balls of his feet. He had a foul odor about him. He had dull, lifeless eyes and long, greasy dirty blonde hair. He was small, no more than five feet six inches tall and one hundred twenty-five pounds. His hair was almost shoulder length, parted in the middle. His eyebrows arched up high over his eyes, and his chin was weak, almost disappearing into a thin-lipped mouth. He had a light mustache encircling his mouth. His eyes were startlingly blue. He was twenty-two years old.

We were in a little interrogation room in the jail area. There were no pictures on the solid white walls, and the only furniture in the room was a small table and two chairs. Donald Sharp stood up against a wall, guarding the door so we wouldn't be interrupted.

I began by introducing myself. I talked to Willie about where he grew up, told him stories about how I had grown up, talked about baseball and a lot of other stuff for over an hour. Then I asked him to pray with me. He listened quietly although he did not bow his head. The prayer went something like this: "God, this nice young man here has got himself involved in some terrible things. I know it wasn't really his fault. It just all got out of hand." I had my hand on his shoulder while I prayed.

Just before the prayer, Willie had signed a consent form, granting us permission to question him. After the prayer, Willie asked me if he was making the news back home. I immediately picked up on his interest. I told him that he was the biggest news that had ever hit Louisiana. He was even bigger that Jesse James. I must have said the magic words, because it was then that Willie began to talk. The story he told made my blood run cold.

"Me and Joe got loaded on some Valiums," he began. "Then we rode around and went to Mandeville. We picked this girl up around 4:30 in the morning. She was walking on the side of the road. I asked her if she wanted a ride. She said yes. So she got in the middle of the seat between us. I asked her where she lived. I told Joe how to get there. Then we pulled over on the side of the road. He got out and I got out and he went to the back of the car and he says, 'Do you know where we can go fuck this whore?' I said, 'She's going to start freaking out, man, if you don't bring her home.' He said, 'Don't worry about it, you know.' And I said, 'I know a place that you can take her.' So we rode around and went up to Fricke's Cave, and Joe blindfolded her and went down in the bottom of the hill. Joe made her lay on the ground and then got his big old knife out and he just cut her throat. He just started jugging her in the throat with it, man. Just jugging her. I mean, jugging her."

I asked him how many times Joe had stabbed her.

"I don't know, man. She had her head lying in his lap. He had her by the hair."

I asked Willie what he was doing while all this horror was going on.

"Freaking out, man. He kept saying, 'This whore ain't dead yet.' I kept telling him, 'Come on man, come on.' He just kept jugging her, man, and then he said, 'We've got to get the fuck out of here.'"

"Did you touch the girl?" I asked.

"I grabbed her hands when she started to get up after he done jugged her in the throat two or three times," Willie said. "I just held her hands, you know. I didn't hold her down."

"What time was the girl killed?" I asked.

"It was around 9 or 10 in the morning," Willie said.

"Where did you pick her up, Robert?" I asked. "Was it in front of the Lakefront Disco?"

"No," he said. "It was by that Corner Pack Store, I believe. By Monroe Street."

"Did Joe rape this girl?" I asked. I hesitated for a moment and then decided that Willie might be more talkative if I used the vulgar terms he was more accustomed to using. This would later make me very uncomfortable when the tape of Willie's confession was played in court. I asked, "Did he fuck her?"

"Yes, he fucked her," Willie said. "She had her pants off before we went down in there. He just laid her down. He says, 'Sit down.' So she sat down. He had her blindfolded."

"What was he using to blindfold her?" I asked.

"A brown bandana," Willie said.

I'm convinced that the reason that Willie and Vaccaro took Faith down that slope in Fricke's Cave blindfolded was not because they didn't want her to know where she was going; it was so that they would not have to look into Faith's eyes. Even hardened criminals like Willie and Vaccaro have a hard time killing if they look directly into their victim's eyes. When a hostage is blindfolded it tells the police that the kidnapper is willing to kill his hostage. The criminal just sees the victim as a thing. The eyes are the windows to their soul.

After he told Donald and me about the murder, I told Willie that I wanted to record his statement or, if he preferred, he could write it all down. He told me that his mother had been arrested, and if I would get her cut loose, he would let me record him. Of course, he had already confessed in detail in my presence and that of Deputy Donald Sharp. I told him that the only thing that I could promise him was that I would get the file, review it for merit personally with the D.A., and if no charges were appropriate, I would see that they were dismissed. I told him that I knew nothing of his mother's case and could not promise him anything in exchange for his confession. I just told him I would not let her be charged for anything that she didn't do. What I told Willie was the truth, and it seemed to satisfy him. He agreed to allow us to record his statement.

After Willie completed his statement, I went back to talk again with Vacarro. I am sure that he thought that Willie would never tell me anything. When I confronted him with the tape recording of Willie's statement, particularly the part where Willie said that Vaccaro had "started jugging her, man, I mean jugging her," he changed his story. As I played Willie's confession, I threw the crime scene photographs down on the table in front of Vaccaro so he could see the horrible damage he and Willie had inflicted on the poor, defenseless Faith.

No longer could he deny any involvement in Faith's murder. However, while Willie blamed Vaccaro for the murder, Vaccaro had a different story to tell.

"I don't even remember picking her up," he said. "All I remember was holding her hands and turning my head the other way. That's all I remember of the whole thing. I don't even know where I was. Like I said, I was full of Valiums. That's why I don't even remember anything about it. All I remember was holding her hands and turning my head the other way. I didn't even see Willie when he cut her."

"Why were you holding her?" I asked.

"I guess so Robert could cut her," Vaccaro said. "I guess so he could cut her throat. He didn't say he was going to cut her throat or anything. He just said, 'Hold her hands.'"

"Was it Robert who cut her," I asked.

"Yeah. I held her hands and turned my head the other way, you know. When we left, I asked him 'Was she dead?' and he said, 'Yeah.' That was it. I don't remember picking her up. The only thing I remember was holding her hands."

After Willie and Vaccaro had given their statements, I called Herb Alexander, one of the assistant prosecutors and a good friend. He said, "Come on, you got to be kidding me. They confessed?" He yelled it across the District Attorney's Office.

I want to comment briefly on the story that Willie and Vaccaro told. Faith Hathaway was a sensible girl, a girl with a sense of purpose in life, a very mature eighteen-year-old. She was not a wild girl, out partying all the time. She rarely dated, rarely stayed out late. She was focused on her life, ready to join the Army, excited about the future. Would she have asked for or voluntarily accepted a ride from Willie and Vaccaro? Absolutely not!

Take a look at the photographs of Willie and Vaccaro and see if anyone in her right mind would have gotten willingly in a truck with them. Add to this the lateness of the hour and the short distance Faith had to walk home, if indeed she was walking home when she came into contact with Willie and Vaccaro.

The Lakefront Disco is only six or seven blocks from Faith's apartment. It fronts on the lake, but is at a corner just a few blocks from Monroe Street, the very street that Faith lived on. If she had been walking, she would have walked straight out the front door of the disco and within a few moments would have been on Monroe Street. She could have walked the whole way in just a few minutes. She would not have needed a ride. But Willie said she was walking, that they picked her up by the side of the road. If she had actually been walking, the distance home would have been laughably short. A ride? No way.

And here is another problem with Willie's story. I asked Willie, "Do you remember what time of the night ya'll got her, picked her up?"

He said, "It was early in the morning, man. It was 4:30 in the morning."

I asked him, "Was it out in front of the Lakefront Theater?"

He said, "Naw. It was by that Corner Pack Store, I believe. By Monroe Street. It's the one that runs in front of Pre-Stressed Concrete, I think. All the way down by that Corner Pack."

So in Willie's own words, he and Vaccaro didn't first encounter Faith at the disco, but on Monroe Street. And at the Corner Pack Store, near Pre-Stressed Concrete.

Pre-Stressed Concrete is almost directly in front of the Monroe Apartments where Faith lived. The Corner Pack Store is only a block from the apartment complex. It is ludicrous that Faith would have accepted a ride from Willie and Vaccaro when she had already made it home, especially at 4:30 in the morning.

And there are other problems with what Willie is saying. First, the last time anyone saw Faith was around 1:30 A.M. So it is almost certain that it wasn't 4:30 in the morning when Faith came under the control of Willie and Vaccaro, but much earlier. Indeed, Willie got three cups of ice at 2:30 A.M. at Jim's Chicken Town, lending support for the theory that she was already with him and Vaccaro by that time.

Second, the Corner Pack Store is on the other side of the Monroe Apartments from the Lakefront Disco. If Faith had been walking home, she would have had to pass her apartment before arriving at the Corner Pack Store. When you add it all up, it is clear that Willie was lying when he claimed that Faith voluntarily got in the truck with Vaccaro and him.

I had not really given one thought to poor Faith's family until I lay down to go to sleep that night. As I had since I was a kid, I said my prayers and asked God to guide me as we pursued the prosecution of Willie and Vaccaro for Faith's murder. I had been told all my life to be kind to people on your way up because you are going to see the same people on the way back down. Before I could finish my prayer, I had a clear sense of what I needed to do. "Help Faith's family as much as you can." A giant burden was lifted from my shoulders. Helping Faith's family was the only thing about any of this that was important. I knew what they wanted. They wanted justice for their little girl, and they were looking at me to make sure they got their justice. With God's help, I knew that I was up to the task.

THE WHEELS OF JUSTICE
BEGIN TO TURN

Within a few weeks of their capture in Arkansas, Robert Willie and Joe Vaccaro pled guilty in federal court to the kidnapping of Mark Brewster and Debbie Cuevas. U.S. District Judge Jack M. Gordon imposed three consecutive life sentences on each of them. The next order of business was for them to be tried in Franklinton for the murder of Faith Hathaway.

Summer descended with a vengeance on Washington Parish that year. Perhaps it was a sign of the heated legal battle that lay ahead that during the last few days of June and the first week of July, the week that Willie and Vaccaro were indicted, only .85 inch of precipitation fell and that was in the form of hail. The highs that week soared, ranging from 95 to 101 degrees. On Monday, June 30, 1980, the Washington Parish Grand Jury indicted Willie and Vaccaro for the first-degree murder and aggravated rape of Faith Hathaway. They were also indicted for the rape of Debbie Cuevas.

On Thursday, July 3, Vaccaro and Willie were transported by federal marshals from New Orleans to Covington for their arraignment in the Twenty-Second Judicial Court before Judge Hillary J. Crain. They arrived at the courthouse at 8:45 A.M. under heavy guard. Deputies cordoned off the courthouse to keep onlookers at a distance. Everyone who entered the courtroom was searched and women's purses were opened. Fourteen deputies and four U.S. marshals stood watch in the courtroom, while two dozen court employees witnessed the fifteen-minute arraignment.

Vaccaro and Willie stood silently beside each other before Judge

Crain as First Assistant District Attorney Herb Alexander read aloud the indictments. Willie was dressed in a blue sweatshirt and brown pants, and he wore sandals. Bond was set at a million dollars each for the rape charges. No bond was set for the murder charges.

District Attorney Marion Farmer led the prosecution team that would seek convictions against Faith Hathaway's killers. He was quoted in the Enterprise, a local newspaper, as saying, "We owe it to the citizens of St. Tammany and Washington parishes to make sure that these two animals do not walk our streets again." This quote would later become a focal point of controversy between the prosecution and the defense and give rise to an extraordinary pre-trial hearing.

Two of Marion's assistants, Bill Alford and Herb Alexander, would bear the actual responsibility for trying the cases against Willie and Vaccaro. Herb was assigned to be the lead prosecutor in the state's case against Robert Willie, while Bill was assigned to prosecute Joe Vaccaro.

Herb, tall, handsome and slightly balding, was a man with an infectious smile and an easy, good humor that rubbed off on everyone he met. Herb occasionally enjoyed wearing a tie covered in American flags. It was Herb's first time to prosecute a first-degree murder case, and he would later say that it was the only one he ever prosecuted in which he felt that the defendant deserved the death penalty. "Willie was a one-man crime wave," Herb said.

"Big Bill" Alford, the man assigned to lead the state's prosecution of Joe Vaccaro, was a giant of a man who had played football at Louisiana State University, and who had worked in the New Orleans District Attorney's Office under District Attorney Jim Garrison. He had been third in command in the New Orleans District Attorney's Office and had prosecuted a large number of capital murder cases, obtaining numerous sentences of death.

Austin McElroy, a lawyer who had been born in Brooklyn, New

York, and grown up on Long Island, New York, was assigned to defend Robert Willie. Austin had practiced law in New York for about ten years, doing mainly criminal defense. However, after attending his tenth law school reunion at Tulane, he decided to move back to Louisiana. For a time, he worked as an Assistant District Attorney under Marion Farmer, who had been a classmate of his at Tulane Law School. After about a year in the D.A.'s office, though, Austin had left to set up his own practice. He also worked part-time at the Public Defender's Office. Austin had handled other murder cases before, but never a death penalty case.

Reggie Simmons, another young lawyer from Washington Parish whose father had once been the mayor of Franklinton, was assigned by the Public Defender's Office to represent Joe Vaccaro. Tom Ford, another local attorney, assisted Reggie in the defense of Joe Vaccaro.

Judge Hillary J. Crain would preside over the trial of Robert Lee Willie. At the time, Judge Crain was the youngest judge ever elected in the state of Louisiana. His reputation was that of honesty and making sure hard-core justice was meted out.

Judge Crain came by his law and order attitude honestly. His grandfather, Robert Wesley Crain, had been killed by two moonshiners in a shootout near the site of a still that he and a fellow deputy, Wiley Pierce, had discovered. The two killers dragged the bodies of the two deputies into a bog where a cow had become mired and died. They stood on the lifeless bodies of the two men, forcing them down into the bog to a depth of about two feet. They then dragged the carcass of the dead cow over the body of Judge Crain's grandfather. One of the killers was sentenced to life in prison but was stabbed to death by another inmate. The other man was sentenced to death and was hanged at the courthouse in Washington Parish on August 31, 1923.

A stone monument to the slain deputies, six feet tall and four feet wide, stands on the south side of the Washington Parish courthouse in Franklinton. It is fitted with a bronze plaque that has the following inscription: "To the sacred memory of Wiley Pierce, born January 10, 1882, and Robert Wesley Crain, born August 16, 1886. Two native born sons of Washington Parish, true and loyal citizens, officers of the law, were foully shot to death while in the performance of a dangerous duty and their bodies brutally tramped into the mud of Betsy's Creek Swamp by illicit distillers of "Moonshine" whisky. Lest we Forget."

Judge A. Clayton James Jr. was set to preside over the trial of Joe Vaccaro.

THE DISTRICT ATTORNEY
ON TRIAL

The sparring between the defense and the state began early in the cases against Robert Willie and Joe Vaccaro. On October 16, before Judge Crain, the lawyers for Willie and Vaccaro sought to have the District Attorney disqualified from prosecuting the cases against them. The principal witness called by the defense was none other than the District Attorney himself, Marion Farmer.

"What is the objective of your duties with regard to criminal matters?" Reggie Simmons asked.

"I think it is to prosecute cases by indictment or by bill of information," District Attorney Marion Farmer said.

"Does your office ever convict defendants of crimes?"

"Hopefully sometimes."

"Is it your desire to obtain convictions of criminal defendants?"

"Well, it is our desire to see justice is done, and that often involves obtaining a conviction, yes."

"Now, specifically regarding the charges against Joseph Vaccaro, have you decided whether or not to try to convict him?" Reggie asked.

"We've decided we have a prosecutable case against Mr. Vaccaro. That's right," Marion said.

"Have you decided whether you will allow Mr. Vaccaro to plea bargain to any lesser offense than first degree murder?"

"I've decided against that, yes."

"Have you decided whether you will allow him to, for instance, plead guilty to first degree murder without capital punishment?"

"I've decided against that."

"If the defendant were to offer to plead guilty right now to second degree murder, which carries a mandatory life sentence, would you allow him to do that?"

"I would not."

"If the defendant were to offer to plead to first degree murder without capital punishment, would you allow him to do that?"

"I would not."

"In other words, you've made up your mind to do everything you can to try him so that you can seek a death penalty verdict, is that correct?" Reggie asked.

"Everything within the bounds of justice, yes," Marion said.

"Mr. Farmer, have you ever said anything defaming or derogatory or demeaning about Joe Vaccaro personally?"

"Other than I would want to see him in prison, that I felt like that we had the evidence to convict him of very serious crimes, if that would be considered demeaning."

"Do you consider Joe Vaccaro to have worth as a human being?" Reggie asked.

"Certainly."

"Do you believe that he deserves to live?"

"Well, I am not sure that I can answer that question. I am going to prosecute him to the fullest extent of the law and whatever the law provides as maximum penalty I am going to ask for that."

"Do you recall referring to the defendants as 'animals'?" Reggie asked.

"I did not use that particular word. I said, 'I am going to make sure these two guys don't walk our streets again.'

"You deny then that you used the term 'animal'?"

"Definitely. I did not use that term," Marion said.

"Do you recall in the newspaper article on June 12 in which Mr. Michael Varnado of your office was quoted as stating that the defendants both confessed, do you recall that?" Reggie asked.

"I've seen that article, yes."

"Did you inquire from him as to whether or not he made any such statement?" Reggie asked.

"Yes. He indicated to me that he hadn't made such a statement," Marion said.

"Do you believe that a plea bargain or a sentence bargain with Joe Vaccaro would hurt you politically?" Reggie asked.

"I don't know. It would be impossible to say. It probably would not help me."

Finally, Herb Alexander had had enough. He objected to the lengthy examination of the district attorney. "We are just going around and around the mulberry bush," he said. Judge Crain agreed.

Next, Reggie called me to the stand. He asked me if I told the newspaper that Willie and Vaccaro had confessed to killing Faith.

I thought back to the day I returned from Arkansas with copies of the statements that Willie and Vaccaro had given. Herb Alexander was impatiently awaiting my return to the District Attorney's Office to hear and read firsthand the horrors that I had only briefly recounted to him on the phone. I was riding in a Washington Parish Sheriff's Office detective's vehicle with Deputy Richard Newman, who had picked me up at the New Orleans International Airport. As we approached the town of Folsom, just a few miles south of Fricke's Cave, we received a radio call, directing Richard to call a particular phone number immediately. It was a Covington phone number. "It might be Marion Farmer," I said.

Richard pulled the cruiser into a grocery store parking lot and up to a pay phone. Richard dialed the number to the urgent anonymous call, then quickly handed me the phone. "It's for you, Varnado," he said. He did not tell me that it was John Fahey from the Enterprise newspaper—the last person in the world I wanted to speak to.

"Mike, I heard you got a confession from Willie and Vaccaro," Fahey said.

"John, please don't say anything about any confession, please," I begged.

"That's all I needed to know!" he said and hung up.

After I explained what had happened, Judge Crain immediately denied the defense motion to disqualify the District Attorney. The trial would proceed as scheduled.

WILLIE'S TRIAL BEGINS

The trial of Robert Willie was set to begin in a basement court-room in the Washington Parish courthouse in the center of Franklinton on Monday, October 20, 1980, just a week short of five months since the murder of Faith Hathaway. At the same time, the trial of Joe Vaccaro was ready to get underway in an upstairs courtroom.

As I pulled up to the rear of the courthouse on that Monday, the smell of death in my car from the crime scene was still faintly detectable. As soon as I shut the door of the cruiser, I breathed in the fresh, fall air as deeply as I could. Above my head, the leaves on the giant, saw-tooth oaks surrounding the courthouse were a vivid mixture of red, gold and yellow. I walked slowly toward the back door of the courthouse, my feet crunching through the huge acorns and dead leaves that carpeted the ground and sidewalk.

For a moment, I remembered that this was the week of the Washington Parish Free Fair, usually one of the highlights of the year for me and for others who live in this part of Louisiana. But not this year—this year I would be praying for and seeking to bring about some measure of justice for Faith Hathaway and her family. I paused by the monument to Judge Crain's grandfather and his fellow deputy who had been murdered by moon-shiners and removed an acorn that had somehow worked its way inside one of my penny loafers and now was lodged. As I lowered my foot, I noticed Willie and Vaccaro entering through the passage of the old jail. Their hands were shackled at their waists, and their legs were bound in chains.

"Varnado, how about a smoke?" Willie said.

Without a word, I reached into my pocket and opened a fresh pack of Marlboros. I lit the smoke and placed it in Willie's mouth. I was amazed at how proficient he was at leaning over slightly and removing the cigarette quickly to his hand.

Willie's trial got underway around 9:00 A.M. After Judge Crain made some preliminary statements about the case and how things were going to proceed, the first order of business was the selection of the jury.

Some of the things the prospective jurors said during the process of jury selection show that even in a murder case, real life intrudes. In response to a question concerning the possibility that the jury would be sequestered—kept away from home overnight—one prospective juror said, "My husband would be home with the children. I don't know what kind of condition I'll find my home when I get home."

Another juror was excused because he said that he would be too distracted because he needed to milk the cows. "I've got to milk them cows twice a day," he said. Judge Crain said, "I understand about those cows."

Another prospective juror's problem was her baby. She said, "I have a three-month old baby. I don't think it would affect my decision or being able to listen or anything, but it would be awfully hard to make arrangements for a three-month old to stay for maybe four or five days." She also had a four-year-old, and her husband was working nights that week. She mentioned her mother and said it wouldn't be "insurmountable." "Oh, my mother would love it," she said.

The most significant issue raised by Judge Crain during jury selection was the prospective jurors' feelings about the death penalty. One by one, each of the potential jurors was interviewed in depth as to his or her most intimate thoughts and beliefs about the death penalty. The cramped quarters in the office-sized courtroom were filled to capacity leaving Faith's stepfather, Vern Harvey, sitting directly behind the defendant, Robert Lee Willie, not six feet away. While the jurors were contemplating and answering the barrage of questions fired at them from the Judge and lawyers, Vern Harvey was contemplating his own views of the death penalty. Coming to a decision as to how he felt about capital punishment, at least for the men accused of killing Faith, had not been a difficult struggle.

Many times he had seen the scene play out in his mind. If the jury acquitted Willie or spared him from the chair, he would at that very moment, stand, point his Navy Colt .45 at the back of Willie's head, ask God for mercy, and blow away the back of Willie's head. He would then calmly lay the Colt on the bench, lower his head and raise his hands. The vision had become so strong in Vern Harvey's mind, it was getting harder and harder for him to ignore.

Indeed, this morning he had paid close attention to the security of the courtroom. He was convinced he could quite easily make his way past the deputies guarding the courtroom with his gun in his trousers. "Maybe tomorrow," he thought. "Why even wait for the verdict?"

As if reading his mind, Elizabeth Harvey, Faith's mother, placed her hand on his thigh and squeezed. Vern relaxed momentarily and once again started listening to the jurors as they spoke.

Jury selection took all morning and all afternoon, although there were numerous breaks during the day. Since Vaccaro's trial was also going on at the same time, I would run upstairs to the courtroom where he was on trial to see how things were going. I knew that once the juries were selected, all of the witnesses, including me, would be unable to enter the courtroom until after we had testified. Lawyers and judges call this restriction on witnesses, the "Rule."

Once, during a break, as I walked across the narrow catwalk that connected the jail and the courthouse, I looked up in time to see Willie on his way back into court. Even though his hands were shackled, he was able to reach up to his mouth and take the cigarette that he had smoked down to the filter. He dropped it onto the tile floor and smashed it under his tennis shoe. He grinned at me as he continued to grind the butt much longer than was necessary.

"What's up, dude?" he said as I approached him and his guards. One thing I'll say for Willie—he never held a grudge against me for my part in his ultimate downfall. He knew I had treated him fairly and always shot straight.

"We're fixing to get started," I responded.

"Yeah, hurry up and get this show on the road," he said. "The food stinks up here."

Willie saw the cigarettes in my pocket and nodded at them. "Give me another smoke, hoss." His constant chain-smoking all morning had left "our" pack of cigarettes empty save one.

"I'll have to go get us another pack," I said.

"Hurry up, dude. Be back before the first break," he ordered.

No doubt about it—Willie was much more concerned about the lack of cigarettes than he was about going on trial for his life. Just as I started to give Robert Willie some unsolicited advice about his demeanor in the courtroom, the bailiff opened the door at the other end of the walk and yelled, "The judge is ready, boys. Let's go."

The next day, Tuesday, October 21, the lawyers began battling in earnest. After Judge Crain made some introductory remarks, he looked over at Herb Alexander and told him to make his opening statement. Herb stood and walked confidently over to stand in front of the jury, looking them each directly in the eyes and speaking deliberately and with purpose. His recitation of the horrific facts of the crime would later take five full pages of the trial transcript. Elizabeth Harvey would later say that one of the most wrenching moments during Herb Alexander's opening statement was when he recited Faith's last words before she died: "Why don't you all go on and let me die by myself?" Herb closed his opening statement by saying, "When this case is over, the State is going to ask for a verdict guilty as charged, first-degree murder, and after the course of the trial is over, the State is going to ask you to return a verdict of death in this case."

After Herb finished his opening statement, Austin rose from his place at the table next to Robert Willie and walked toward the jury box. Looking at the members of the jury who would decide the fate of his client, Austin made a brief opening statement.

"Ladies and gentlemen, I can tell just by looking at you what Mr. Alexander told you has shocked you. I can only ask you at this time that you promise yourself that you will not let the shocking aspects of the evidence in this case cloud your minds with all the evidence in this case. I sincerely ask you at this time to promise yourself that. This is extremely important. We are here for a fair trial, and to get a fair trial, we have to have you consider all the evidence in this case, and that's all I'm asking you at this time is you give us a fair trial. Thank you."

Herb first called two of the picnickers who had found Faith's clothing and other personal effects in Fricke's Cave. After they testified, he called L. M. James, the radio operator at the Sheriff's Office. The next witness was Elizabeth Harvey, Faith Hathaway's mother. The electricity in the courtroom was palpable. The jury sat still and erect as Elizabeth Harvey walked slowly to the witness stand.

A Mother's Grief

Herb began his examination of Elizabeth slowly, allowing her to gain some measure of comfort on the witness stand before the difficult task of talking about Faith's death began. After asking Mrs. Harvey to state her name and address, Herb established that she was married to Vernon Harvey, a union carpenter, and that she was the manager of the Monroe Street Apartments where she lived.

"Do you have any children?" Herb asked.

"I had two daughters."

Herb paused. "How many daughters do you have now?"

Mrs. Harvey sat erect and spoke in a deliberate voice. "One daughter."

With this one brief question and answer, a chill went through the courtroom. In a way that was not tangible to the jury before, they now saw and felt the first inkling of the grief and tragedy visited upon the family of Faith Hathaway. Here sitting before them was the mother of a dead girl, allegedly murdered by the skinny young man sitting only a few feet away from them.

Herb Alexander continued. "What are the names of your two daughters?"

"Faith Colleen Hathaway, Lizabeth Dale Harvey."

Mrs. Harvey testified that Faith had turned eighteen in December.

Herb asked, "In May of this year, had she made any plans after graduation from high school?"

"She had plans." A simple sentence—she had plans—but it spoke volumes. Here was the mother of a dead girl, but she was more than a name, she had been a living, vibrant eighteen-year-old. She had plans. My God, Elizabeth Harvey must have thought, she had plans.

"All right. What kind of plans?"

"After graduation, she planned to go into the Army. She was supposed to leave Mandeville on May 28."

The courtroom was hushed as Mrs. Harvey continued to testify. She told the jury how Faith had left home for work around 4:30 P.M. on May 27. She said that Faith was dressed in a blue skirt and a blue blouse and was wearing sandals. She was carrying her purse with her, her cosmetic case, and a paperback book.

Herb showed Mrs. Harvey the sandals, the skirt, the contact case, the purse, the billfold, the driver's license, a billfold-size birth certificate, and a paperback romance novel that had been found in Fricke's Cave. She identified all of them as belonging to Faith. Mrs. Harvey also identified a blouse that Herb showed her.

Mrs. Harvey said, "I washed it many times, sir." After several questions referring only to items of evidence as an exhibit number, here now was a blouse that had belonged to Faith before it became Exhibit 11. Elizabeth Harvey knew this because she had washed this item many times.

Herb was ready now to take the examination of Mrs. Harvey to a different level. He began to ask her to identify items that had not been found by the picnickers. Rather, these items had been found on Faith's decomposing body, although the jury would not find this out until later. The first item that Herb showed Mrs. Harvey was a ring.

"It is my daughter's ring," she said. Here was Faith's mother holding a ring that had once been hers, and that she had given to her daughter to wear. Now, in front of all these people she was identifying it as Exhibit 12 in a murder trial.

"How did she get that ring?"

"She liked it. She asked me for it, and I gave it to her."

"You are positive that is her ring."

"Yes, sir. I bought it at Gordon's Jewelers. A seven-day wishing ring."

"Now I show you what has been marked for purposes of identification as State versus Willie 13 and ask you if you can identify that?"

"Yes, sir. It's my daughter's watch."

"Are you positive?"

"Yes, sir. It has a blue face and points at each end. I just had the band put on at Christmas time." Again, Elizabeth Harvey took an item of evidence, a watch marked impersonally as Exhibit 13, and put a personal note on it. It wasn't just a piece of evidence, it was an unusual watch that Faith had worn and enjoyed, that had gotten a new band just last Christmas.

"I'm going to open up what has been numbered for purposes of identification as State versus Willie 14, and ask you to look at that, if you would please."

"It doesn't have the same look because it was a very bright color. But it is the same shape and has the same writing on it as a necklace my daughter got with her graduation announcements."

"Did she wear anything like that, Mrs. Harvey?"

"She wore it from the day she received it, and her announcements went out."

"Announcements of what?"

"Her graduation."

"Where did she wear it, ma'am?"

"Around her neck. She wore it all the time, constantly."

"Mrs. Harvey, I'm going to show you what I'm going to mark for purposes of identification as State versus Willie 15 and ask you if you recognize this, ma'am?"

"Yes."

"What is that?"

"It's a portion of a picture of my daughter receiving her diploma," Mrs. Harvey said. This photograph had a special meaning to her because it had been displayed over Faith's closed casket, which itself had been draped in an American flag.

"All right, and what does it show in the frontal area right here around her neck?"

"Her necklace that she wore that she received with her graduation announcements."

"One similar to the one that has been marked for purposes of identification as State versus Willie 14?"

"That is what you said."

"Thank you. Do you know how much money your daughter was carrying when she left home that evening?"

"She had about fifteen dollars with her that particular evening, but she was to be paid."

"Do you know how much she was to get paid?"

"I know how much she said that she thought she was going to get paid."

"How much?"

At this point, Austin objected. Judge Crain sustained the objection, noting that the question called for hearsay.

"Now I show you what has been marked for purposes of identification as State's exhibit 16, Mrs. Harvey, and ask you if you can identify that and if so how?"

"This is the key to my apartment."

"Who had keys to your apartment, Mrs. Harvey?"

"My daughter, my husband and myself."

"Did your daughter live with you in the same house, Mrs. Harvey?"

"No, sir. She didn't."

"Where did she live?"

"She lived in the Monroe Apartments at Apartment number 28."

"Did you see her—how often did you see your daughter?"

"Very frequently."

"How far is that from where you live, the Monroe Apartments?"

"I live in the Monroe Apartments."

"How far away from you did she live?"

"It's about two hundred yards."

"After May 27, when was the next time you saw your daughter?"

"From when, sir?"

"After May 27, 1980, when was the next time you saw your daughter?"

"I never have, sir." This line fell like a bomb in the courtroom. Here was Elizabeth Harvey, who had just identified seventeen exhibits as items all belonging to her daughter, Faith. And the last thing the jury heard was that Faith had walked out of her life one spring afternoon and had never returned. Surely the members of the jury had a personal chill, thinking about their own children and grandchildren. But still there had been almost no mention of Robert Willie or what had happened to Faith. All the jury knew, other than what the lawyers had told them in their opening statements, was that Faith had left on May 27 and had never been seen again, and that a group of picnickers had found her purse and clothing in Fricke's Cave. But it wouldn't be long before the link between Faith's disappearance and Robert Willie was made.

Herb continued. "What did you do? Say, on May 28 or May 29?"

"Well, on May 28, when my daughter did not come for me, we were going to check over to make sure of the list, she had everything with her. She was to leave, her recruiting sergeant was to meet her at my home."

"And where was she going?"

"To New Orleans. She was supposed to report to New Orleans."

"What did you do when she didn't show up?"

"At 4 P.M., I called her recruiting sergeant. He had been by the apartment two times before."

"And what did you do after you talked to her recruiting sergeant?"

"At 6:00 P.M., I called the Mandeville Police Department."

"And what did you do when you called the Mandeville Police Department?"

"I had my husband call the Mandeville Police Department for me."

"For what reason, ma'am?"

"Because she was supposed to have been over in New Orleans by that time, no later than that. Earlier."

At this point, Herb tendered the witness to Austin McElroy. Questioning a victim's mother is always tricky. The jury feels a great deal of sympathy for someone like Mrs. Harvey. In addition, all that had been established is that the items found at Fricke's Cave belonged to Faith, and that Faith did not show up as expected on May 28. There was nothing really of importance that Austin could have gained from cross-examining Mrs. Harvey. He did the prudent thing and announced that he had no questions.

My Turn on the Witness Stand

It was now time for Herb to move the case to the next level. He had to present evidence of Faith's murder and connect Robert Willie to the murder. This was a crucial moment in the trial. If the prosecution failed to make the connection well, Willie might walk free. I was called to be that crucial witness.

I had been waiting in the hallway since Judge Crain had invoked the "Rule," sequestering the witnesses. Now I heard my name called and I walked quickly to the door of the courtroom and entered. All eyes were on me, from Judge Crain in the front of the courtroom to Robert Lee Willie, sitting beside his lawyer. Herb Alexander stood near the witness chair, waiting for me.

I strode to the witness stand and took the oath to tell the truth, the whole truth and nothing but the truth. It was time to do my part to seek justice for Faith Hathaway, her family and all of us. I looked briefly at Robert Lee Willie. He smirked and waited.

After a few preliminary questions, Herb got to the heart of the matter. "Did you have occasion to become involved in an investigation around the area of Fricke's Cave?"

"Yes, sir. I did."

"Would you tell the jury when you first became involved in that investigation, please?"

I was about to answer when Austin McElroy jumped to his feet and objected. "Would the court instruct the witness not to read from a prepared statement?"

I did have my notes with me so that I would be able to get all the dates correct now that it was about five months since Faith's murder. I had noted the date that Faith's belongings were found (the afternoon of Sunday, June 1), the date that Debbie was freed (Sunday morning, June 1, around 8:00 A.M.), the date that I received the call from Richard Newman about Faith's belongings having been found (Monday, June 2), the date I went to Fricke's Cave to search after dark (Tuesday, June 3), the date I found Faith's body (around noon on Wednesday, June 4), and the date that I went to Arkansas to interview Willie and Vaccaro (Tuesday, June 10).

But I can tell you that I needed no notes to remember all the gruesome details of finding Faith's body. That is a horrible memory that I will never be able to erase from my mind. Robert Willie was smirking at me again. He seemed actually to be enjoying this.

Judge Crain shook his head. "He can refresh his memory if he's got notes he's made. Do you need that to refresh your memory?"

I nodded and told Judge Crain that I needed my notes only for dates. I have always been able to recall the details of all the cases I have handled, but I have sometimes forgotten little things, such as where I left my keys this morning. I did not want a minor lapse in my recall over a date to present a problem for the prosecution of Robert Willie.

Judge Crain nodded. "OK. If you do, you're going to have to let the defendant's counsel see it. Do you want to see it, Mr. McElroy?"

Austin said, "Yes, I'd like to, yes." So the bailiff handed my notes to Austin who took a few moments to look over them. I wonder if he could even read my handwriting. If so, it did not matter to me. There was nothing in my notes that was untrue or that Austin and Robert Willie did not already know. Still, Austin was putting up a good fight for Willie. I appreciate that. All criminal defendants are entitled to a zealous defense. I want them to have the best defense possible. I believe fervently in our criminal justice system, and I want no less than the best defense for anyone accused of a crime, particularly when a life is on the line.

After Austin looked over my notes, he seemed satisfied and handed them back to the bailiff who gave them back to me. I then began to tell how I had found Faith's body.

I first mentioned that I had gone out to Fricke's Cave on Tuesday by myself to look for Faith's body. I told how I searched by myself for forty-five minutes to an hour before it got dark. I then told how I had gone back the next day, Wednesday, June 4, about noon to search again, accompanied by Brian Lynch.

Herb asked me to tell the jury what happened.

"I got to the Cave, I'd say, around twelve noon, and I started searching the area," I said. "I met some deputies coming out of that area and they described as best they could where Faith's clothing had been found. From the spot where Faith's clothing had been found I started searching the area further down in the swamp where the rest of the searchers had been searching. I went down into the swamp and I began to smell something and I just kept making circles. Brian Lynch and I kept making circles. About a hundred feet off the trail, I walked right up onto the spot where her body was lying."

Herb Alexander at this point handed a photograph to me that had been marked as Exhibit 17. It was a photograph of poor Faith's decaying corpse. He asked, "I'd like to ask you if this is an accurate representation of what you discovered, the body you discovered down in the Fricke's Cave area on June 4, 1980?"

It was horrible. I looked at Robert Willie and then said slowly, "Yes, sir. That photograph accurately depicts what I found."

Herb then showed me one more photograph, Exhibit 18, which also was a photograph of Faith's body, and I identified that photograph as well.

I continued with my testimony. "The first thing I did was to secure the area, and I had Brian call the Sheriff's Office and notify the State Police Crime Lab to come to the scene. I began looking around the area. I waited. I didn't do anything to the crime scene until the Louisiana State Police Crime Lab got there. I called Mr. Farmer, Mr. Alford, and the coroner."

I then told the jury how I took the seven-day wishing ring that Elizabeth Harvey had earlier identified off of the ring finger of Faith's left hand. I also told the jury that I removed from Faith's left wrist the blue-faced Timex watch with the new band that Elizabeth Harvey had purchased just the previous Christmas.

After I told how Faith's body had been removed from the scene by the ambulance service and the funeral director with my help and the help of some deputies, Herb said he was finished with his examination. Since all that had been established was that Faith was found dead in Fricke's Cave, there was little that Austin McElroy could ask me that would help his client. He did the prudent thing and asked me no questions.

I walked down from the witness stand. Since I knew that I would be recalled as a witness when it came time to play Willie's confession for the jury, I returned to the hallway to smoke a cigarette and wait.

THE FIRST FINGER OF
ACCUSATION

At this point, the jury knew that Faith Hathaway had disappeared in the early morning hours of Wednesday, May 28, and that she had been found dead and decomposing in Fricke's Cave on the following Wednesday, June 4. I noticed several of the jurors throwing fleeting glances at Robert Willie. Just who was the young man sitting there so calmly? When would they hear about him? It would not be long now.

The trial was proceeding quickly. We had started that morning, and it was now around noon. Judge Crain called a recess for lunch until 1:30 p.m. He told the jury that the Sheriff's Office would get them some sandwiches

After lunch, court reconvened. The first witness was Julius Spell, who had been in the trucking and gravel business for approximately twenty years in Washington and St. Tammany Parishes. He would also be the first witness to testify directly about Robert Willie.

Herb asked him, "Do you know anybody by the name of Robert Lee Willie?"

The jury snapped to attention. Here, at last, was the first connection between the murder of Faith Hathaway and the young man sitting quietly in the courtroom by his lawyer only a few feet away from them.

Julius Spell did not glance at Robert Willie. "Yes, I do."

"Do you see him in the courtroom?" Herb asked.

Julius Spell pointed at Robert Lee Willie. "Let the record

reflect that the witness had indicated the defendant, Robert Lee Willie, seated at the left end of counsel table," Herb said.

Julius Spell then went on to testify that he had known Robert Lee Willie for several years and that Willie had worked for him for a few months as a truck driver back in 1977, hauling gravel.

"Where were you pumping gravel at the time he was working for you?" Herb asked.

"Behind Fricke's Cave down on the river. About a half a mile from Fricke's Cave."

"To go to the gravel pit that you were working, would you use the same gravel road that leads to Fricke's Cave?"

"Yes, same one."

"Would you say that he was familiar with that area?" Herb asked.

Julius Spell shook his head affirmatively. "Yes."

After Herb sat down, Austin McElroy rose from his chair. Now that Robert Willie had been at least indirectly connected to the murder of Faith Hathaway by virtue of his knowledge of Fricke's Cave, Austin needed to not allow the State to have the last word with Julius Spell.

Austin approached Mr. Spell. "How may other employees of yours worked in the Fricke's Cave area?"

Julius Spell at first did not give a very direct answer. "Oh, that would be hard for me to say."

Austin pressed him. "A good number of people?"

"Sure," he acknowledged.

Austin had made his point. Robert Lee Willie was not the only person working in the Fricke's Cave area. Indeed, there were many people with the same familiarity with the Cave as he had. "I have no further questions," Austin said.

THE BUG MAN

Julius Spell was followed to the witness stand by the coroner, Dr. Jerry Thomas, and by a number of law enforcement officers, including Deputy Richard Newman, all of whom confirmed how Faith's body had been discovered and the condition in which I found it. He then called Diane Baham, who lived on the highway between Fricke's Cave and Covington. She testified that she found a red and white shirt lying on the side of the road across from the driveway of her home.

Herb asked Diane Baham to describe the shirt, which was held up for the jury to see. "The sleeves were torn and the belt has been torn out of the seams and the buttons were as if it had been pulled out."

"Was it just this way when you found it?"

"It was this way."

"Were there any buttons on this shirt when you found it?"

Diane shook her head no.

This was the same shirt that Mrs. Harvey had said belonged to Faith and which she knew because she had washed it so many times before. This was the shirt that Faith changed into after work and before she went to the Lakefront Disco. This shirt had been found on the side of the road between Fricke's Cave and Covington.

Herb next asked Judge Crain to allow him to pass the shirt to the jury for their inspection. The jury passed the shirt among themselves, studying the rips and tears and the missing buttons.

Richard Newman was recalled to the stand. Herb Alexander had failed to establish a key point—that the evidence, the purse, the clothing, all the other personal effects of Faith Hathaway, had always been in police custody with no unknown persons having control of them from the time they had been found. This is called establishing a "chain of custody" and it is necessary in criminal cases. It is just this problem with the chain of custody that became an issue in the case against O.J. Simpson with respect to the collection of blood samples.

So Herb asked Richard where things had been kept and who had had control over them in the months since the murder. The answer was that the evidence had been locked up at the Sheriff's Office, except when it had been sent off to the State Crime Lab in Baton Rouge.

"You took it yourself?" Herb asked.

"Yes, sir."

All of the physical evidence was transported personally by Richard Newman to Baton Rouge or kept in the Sheriff's Office until it was turned over to the District Attorney's Office. After Richard established the chain of custody, Herb passed the witness, but Austin had no questions.

The next witness called by the state was Dr. Lamar Meeke, one of the most unusual and interesting witnesses in the entire trial of Robert Lee Willie.

Dr. Chester Lamar Meeke was an associate professor in the Department of Entomology at Louisiana State University. Asked to explain the field of entomology to the jury, Dr. Meeke said, "Entomology is just the study of insects, not only the biology but the ecology and all the other aspects of science that deals with insects."

What was the jury thinking at this point? Why was an entomologist testifying in a murder trial here in Franklinton, Louisiana? Perhaps some of them had an idea. They would all soon find out.

After stating that he taught a course at LSU in medical ento- mology that covers blowflies and other flies that are associated with living and dead tissue, Herb Alexander tendered Dr. Meeke to the court as an expert witness. If the court accepted Dr. Meeke as an expert, Herb would be allowed to ask Dr. Meeke to give his opinions in addition to testifying merely to facts—one of the great advantages for an expert witness.

Austin McElroy had no objection to Dr. Meeke's status as an expert witness and so Judge Crain accepted Dr. Meeke's creden- tials as establishing him as an expert in entomology.

Herb got right to the point. "Dr. Meeke, did you have some maggots sent to you in this case?"

"Yes. The criminal laboratory in Baton Rouge sent some fly larvae to me."

"Explain to the jury, please, the stages that a blowfly goes through," Herb said.

Dr. Meeke cleared his throat, looked directly at the jury and began. "Flies have what we call a complete life cycle: they have an egg, a maggot or larvae stage, a pupae, and an adult. The maggot stage of blowflies may last anywhere from four to seven days, and this is in addition to the one day the egg takes to develop. After the maggot matures, it goes into somewhat of a resting stage— what we call the pupae, and this pupae stage is no longer associ- ated with the body. It's found in the soil itself, in close association to the rotting carcass, and the pupae stage will take approximately three or four days to mature. The adult will then emerge from this pupae case and begin its free existence in nature. That is the fly that we see flying around in the room and other places in nature."

Herb next began to question Dr. Meeke specifically about the fly maggots that the State Police Crime Lab had sent him to examine. Herb asked, "Would you tell the jury approximately how old you thought the blowfly larvae were?"

"Well, there were several stages of the larvae that we received. The larvae stage goes through four different growth stages in the maggot stage and each stage gets a little bit bigger. The container that we received had different stages in it, but the ones that were the most mature were probably five days old. These five days include the time they spent in the egg stage, so we figured that the flies came in contact with the body from which these larvae had been removed approximately five days earlier."

Herb wanted to know how long after death the five-day period would begin. "Is it necessary that the breeding start as soon as the body expires? In other words, if it's animal or human and it expires, is it automatic that the blowflies are going to start breeding on that body immediately?"

Dr. Meeke answered, "There is a lag time in which it takes the adult female mosquito or fly to deposit her larvae or her eggs on the body. That period varies according to the condition of the body. If there are any open wounds, the attraction that the fly has to those locations is speeded up."

Herb next focused on questions dealing with human victims of crime and the relationship between time of death and the development of maggots.

"Let's assume it's a human body, what are the first areas that the blowfly would tend to lay its eggs in?"

"The female fly is attracted to any food source that is in a liquid formulation, like if there were any drainage to the face, the nose, the head, around the eyes—these are the areas she will generally lay her eggs first."

"Alright. If the eyes were open, would that be an area that would be lucrative?" Herb asked.

"Definitely," Dr. Meeke said.

"If the nasal passages were open, would that be an area that would attract them?" Herb continued, his line of questioning focusing in turn on each of the areas of Faith's body ravaged by the maggots, as shown in Exhibits 17 and 18.

"That is correct," Dr. Meeke said.

Pausing for emphasis and looking directly at the jury, Herb asked, "If the mouth were open, would that be an area that would attract them?"

"It would."

"If the body were unclothed, nude, if it was a female, would the vagina be one of the areas that the black blowfly would be attracted to?"

"Yes, definitely so."

"How about the anal passage?"

"Very much so. Probably more so than the head area."

"Now if there were open wounds anywhere on the body that had bled prior to death, in relationship to the other areas I've named, how much more prone would it be to go into a wound area?"

"I think probably much more so initially than the head area if there were no wounds or open lesions to the head."

Herb was now ready to tie the ends together. He showed Dr. Meeke a photograph, Exhibit 17. He asked Dr. Meeke to look at the area depicted in the photograph just below the neck area and to describe what it showed.

"It appears to be a large accumulation of eggs and fly larvae in around the clavicle of the neck area of the victim."

"In regular language, that's what a lot of people would refer to as maggot infestation, is it not?" Herb asked.

"That's correct," Dr. Meeke answered. "I have seen a color slide which showed a lateral view of the body, and I did note the extreme number of larvae, or maggots, associated with the chest area and also the vaginal area."

"I ask you to direct your attention to the right hand depicted and ask if the condition of that hand would indicate anything particular to you about this particular body?" Herb asked.

"It looks like the skin has been cut and opened up in comparison to the whole structure of the other hand and the slides that I have seen in the past with various views of the body showed maggots associated with the right hand."

Herb ended his examination of Dr. Meeke by asking him if the condition of Faith's right hand showed that it had been injured so as to cause bleeding.

"Well, that is entirely possible. The tissue that was associated with the hand was completely devoid due to the maggot infestation in the hand as compared to the other hand."

Herb thanked Dr. Meeke for his testimony, and after he left the stand, the jury could see that a couple of additional pieces to the puzzle had been put in place. First, if there had been any doubt before, it was now clear that Faith's body had been savaged as shown by the massive maggot infestation in her many wounds. And, thanks to the expertise of a "bug man," the approximate date of Faith's death had been established—a date that was consistent with her murder by Willie and Vaccaro. Thanks to the science of entomology, it had been shown that Faith had died before the kidnapping of Mark and Debbie, a time when Willie and Vaccaro had no alibi.

THE PATHOLOGIST

Herb tied up a few loose ends, and then he asked that all of the exhibits that had been admitted into evidence be passed to the jury. It was a somber moment for everyone there as the twelve jurors and two alternates sitting in the jury box passed the last belongings of a murdered girl. Did they feel like eavesdroppers or voyeurs, sifting through a dead person's things, sitting comfortably in a bright courtroom on a beautiful fall day, while the owner's body lay smoldering in the grave? For a jury to actually touch the evidence of a crime is a moment of high drama in a trial, and it must have been an uncomfortable moment for Robert Lee Willie to watch these men and women who were charged with determining his fate studying and weighing in their hands the very items that he had ripped from Faith Hathaway on that faraway dawn in Fricke's Cave.

After the jury had passed Faith's personal items among themselves, it was time to continue. At this point, very little had been said about how Faith had died. This piece of the puzzle was about to be put into place for the jury. Herb called Dr. Paul McGarry to the witness stand.

Dr. Paul McGarry was a professor of pathology at the LSU School of Medicine and the pathologist for the coroner's office in New Orleans. He testified that one of the duties of his office was to perform autopsies. Dr. McGarry testified that on Thursday, June 5, the day after I discovered Faith's body in Fricke's Cave, he performed the autopsy on Faith's body. He spoke calmly and in measured tones about the most horrific of sights.

"The body was that of a young white female measuring about five feet five inches," he began. "The weight of the body I estimated at about one hundred and thirty. The hair was light brown. The hair was partly separated as occurs after death. I estimated that the body had been dead about a week before the autopsy was done."

Dr. McGarry paused for a moment, before continuing. "There was extensive tissue loss I attributed mainly to the activity of the parasites that were on the body. The maggots partially destroyed some of the soft tissue. There was a large, slash-like opening in the soft tissues in the front of the neck extending all the way across the neck, which was also filled with maggots and had a dark brown discoloration on its edges. I felt that this was probably the fatal wound. This looked like a deep cutting type of wound in the front of the neck."

The jury sat rapt as Dr. McGarry continued his morbid review of the state of Faith's body. "There was extensive bloating and expansion of the body tissues, and the skin was discolored, brownish and dry, that part of the skin that had not been involved with the maggots. There was an injury of the right hand, which had extended deeply into the thumb and the index finger, and the bones of the fingers were exposed and partly missing. I interpreted this as a deep wound of the right hand, and probably representing a defense wound. The genital organs were also involved by extensive maggot activity, and there was a laceration of the lining of the vagina of the kind that is seen as a result of forceful intercourse."

Herb Alexander wanted to fix the jury's attention on the rape that he was attempting to prove since rape was one of the aggravating factors that would support a decision by the jury to impose the death penalty. "Did you examine the interior of the vagina on the body?"

"Yes."

"You said it had a jagged tear, are those your words?" Herb asked.

"Yes."

"Approximately what was the size of that tear?"

"The tear was about an inch long," Dr. McGarry said. "This is the type tear that is frequently seen in the front part of the vagina in women who have had forceful intercourse. We see this frequently in rape cases."

Herb anticipated that the defense might attempt to blame the tear in the vagina on the maggot activity throughout the body. He asked, "Had the maggots interfered in any way with the tear in the vagina?"

Dr. McGarry was confident in his response. "The tear was very clear. It was not dissolved away by the maggot activity."

Again, Herb attempted to cut off potential defense arguments on the lack of seminal evidence. He asked, "Did the maggot infestation in the interior of the vagina have any effect on seminal fluid that might have been left there, spermatozoa that might have been left there?"

"Yes, that plus the post-mortem interval would tend to cause the spermatozoa to disappear," Dr. McGarry said.

Herb next turned to a discovery made by Dr. McGarry during his autopsy that added a note of additional poignancy to the testimony.

"During the course of your autopsy when you were examining the neck area, Dr. McGarry, did you discover anything there that you removed from the neck area of the body?"

Dr. McGarry nodded. "I examined the hyoid bone, which is the little delicate neck bone which surrounds or extends above the throat and in front of the throat, and it was partially disconnected. It was not fractured. There was a little chain, a little gold chain with a pendant on it."

Herb showed Dr. McGarry Exhibit 4, a clear plastic envelope with a brown envelope in it containing a medallion and chain.

"This is the one I removed because I described the printing on the pendant, which is '*Class of 80*' and '*Dawn of New Decade.*' That's the pendant I removed."

THE JURY HEARS
WILLIE'S CONFESSION

The next several witnesses established that Joe Vaccaro had borrowed a large hunting knife from a friend of his and Willie's about two weeks before Faith's murder, and that the FBI had found the knife at the home of Sterling Durache, a friend of Willie's and a person who allowed Willie to stay with him.

The moment of truth was approaching. It was now time to connect Willie to the murder of Faith Hathaway. The witness who would do this was Donald Sharp, a sergeant in the St. Tammany's Sheriff's Office. "Do you know Robert Willie?" Herb asked.

"Yes, sir." He pointed at Willie. "Sitting right there with the green shirt on."

"On or about June 9 or 10, did you have occasion to go to Arkansas?"

"Yes, sir. I did. Texarkana Police Department, Texarkana, Arkansas."

"Who did you go with?"

"Mike Varnado of the D.A.'s office, Richard Newman of the Washington Parish Sheriff's Office, Walter Smith of the Louisiana State Police and Ronnie Pierce of the Louisiana State Police. We were going up there to question Robert Willie and Joseph Vaccaro regarding the murder of Faith Hathaway."

"Did you have occasion to see Robert Willie while you were there?"

"Yes, sir. I did."

"Who else was present when you spoke to him?"

"Mike Varnado and Richard Newman."

Donald recalled that we had interviewed Willie on the afternoon of June 10. He testified that he informed Willie of his constitutional rights before the questioning of him began. Herb carefully walked Donald through the questions designed to show that Willie had been informed of his rights against self-incrimination and his right to have an attorney, and that Willie had understood his rights and had waived them. He continued. "Did you or anyone in your presence offer him anything of value such as immunity from prosecution or any other favor to get him to make a statement?"

"No, sir."

"Did you or anyone in your presence threaten, coerce, intimidate or physically abuse Robert Lee Willie to get him to make a statement?"

"No, sir."

"What kind of condition was he in that you observed?"

"Seemed to me like he was in good condition. He understood everything we explained to him. At least he said he did."

"To the best of your appreciation, did you feel that he did?" Herb asked.

"Yes, sir," Donald Sharp said.

Now for the moment of truth. "Did he in fact make a statement in your presence?"

"Yes, sir."

"What kind of statement was it?"

"He made an oral statement first. Then he made an oral statement that we taped."

Not long after Donald Sharp testified, Judge Crain ordered a recess in the trial so that he could meet with Willie and his lawyer and Herb Alexander for the State to discuss Willie's statement and how it was going to be presented to the jury. At this point, all the jury knew was that Willie had made a statement. The jury had no idea what the statement contained. They were about to find out, but first questions remained as to whether the kidnapping and rape of Debbie Cuevas and the attempted killing of Mark Brewster would be included in the statement the jury would hear. Typically, juries are not allowed to know about other crimes of a defendant. So, Judge Crain wanted to carefully address with Willie what his viewpoint was about the statement.

Judge Crain was all business. "Mr. Willie, step over here. I have been over this confession that you gave to the deputies, and I have indicated to your attorney that there are two areas I would mark out of the confession. One is contained on page seven, and I have the brackets in pencil. Your attorney has indicated to me you might want to keep this in, and I want you to make a specific determination now as to whether you want it in. I will order it out unless you specifically request it in. Question: 'Was the girl obviously dead when you left?' Answer: 'If I would have killed her, I would have killed the other one, you know, Debbie, because she looked, the chick looked all right, too, but I just can't be killing chicks, man.' Question: 'Who wanted to kill Debbie?' Answer: 'Joe and Tommy.'

Willie turned to his lawyer and asked what he thought. Austin said to Willie, "You have to make the request."

Willie, in character for him, said, "Do whatever you want. It don't matter to me."

Judge Crain ordered it out.

Willie and his counsel and the prosecutor all filed back into the courtroom. The bailiff called court into session and, as everyone stood, Judge Crain returned to the bench. He asked that the jury be brought back into court. Once the members of the jury had taken their seats in the jury box, Ronnie Pierce was called to the stand. After he testified briefly as to our trip to Texarkana, it was time for me to drive the final nail into the coffin.

Herb said in a firm voice, "The State calls Detective Mike Varnado to the stand."

I entered the courtroom and walked quickly to the witness chair. After being reminded that I was still under oath, I took a deep breath and waited for Herb to begin his questioning. I glanced over at the jury. They were focused and sitting still, waiting to finally hear what Robert Lee Willie had said about the killing of Faith Hathaway.

I told the jury that when I arrived at the jail in Texarkana, I had interviewed both Robert Lee Willie and Joe Vaccaro in connection with the murder of Faith Hathaway.

Herb asked, "Who did you interview first?"

I said that I had interviewed Joe Vaccaro first.

"Did he indicate to you any involvement in this matter at that time?" Herb asked.

"No, sir."

Next, Herb asked me about my questioning of Robert Willie. I told how I had obtained Willie's written consent to submit to questioning, that he had read the form and had indicated that he understood his rights.

Herb asked, "Did you tell him that he had a right to talk to a lawyer for advice before he was asked any questions and that he could have the lawyer with him during questioning?"

"Yes, sir," I said.

"Did he indicate he understood that right?"

"He did."

"Did he indicate he wanted a lawyer during the time he was questioned?" Herb asked.

"He indicated he did not," I said.

Next Herb walked me through the laundry list of questions concerning Willie's statement and the fact that it had been given voluntarily. Had I offered him immunity, reduction of sentence, reduction of charge or anything of value in order to get the statement?

"Of course not," I said.

Had I threatened Willie or abused him?

My answer was simple: "Certainly not. No, sir."

Was Willie under the influence of alcohol or drugs?

"No, he was not."

I next told how the first statement that Willie gave was oral.

That is, we were just talking. I was asking questions, and he was answering, but no recording of the statement was made.

"After the oral statement was finished, did you take another statement from him?"

"Yes, sir. I did. I took a taped statement."

The moment of truth was at hand.

"Do you have that taped statement in your possession?"

"I do," I said.

"After the taped statement was taken, what was done with it?"

"It was transcribed by one of the secretaries at the police department the next morning, June 11."

Herb showed the transcript of Willie's statement, which was marked as Exhibit 22.

"Yes, sir. This is the statement I took."

"How do you recognize it?"

"Well, of course, he signed the bottom of every page and also went through it and made some corrections."

"Did he read that before he signed it?"

"Yes, sir."

"And there are pen and ink corrections notated thereon?"

"Yes, sir."

"Who made those?"

"Robert Willie."

"In his own handwriting?"

"Yes, sir."

"Did he sign each page of that while you were present?"

"Yes, sir. He did."

After a brief cross-examination, the jury was excused and Austin objected to the playing of Willie's taped confession. He argued that since Willie initially upon being arrested in Arkansas had stated that he wished to speak to an attorney, he should not have been questioned until he had seen an attorney. He also argued that the State had not proved that a crime had been committed. In other words, Austin was arguing that the State had not shown that Faith had been killed as a result of the commission of a crime.

Judge Crain noted that Willie had voluntarily waived his right to speak with an attorney. He also noted that there had been sufficient evidence to find that Faith had died as the result of a crime. Judge Crain ordered the tape recording of Willie's statement played for the jury while the members of the jury followed along with copies of the transcription, the same one signed and corrected by Robert Willie.

As Robert Lee Willie's slow, deliberate drawl filled the courtroom, the jury sat stone still. I watched closely as Willie said that Vaccaro had "jugged" Faith time and again with the knife.

Now the circle was complete. The jury knew that Faith was dead and that Robert Willie and Joe Vaccaro had killed her. The jury heard the same story that Robert Lee Willie had told me. They heard how Faith had been picked up and taken to Fricke's Cave. They heard how she had been taken blindfolded and nude down the steep embankment into the heavily wooded gorge just as day was breaking. They heard how she was forced to lie down on her jeans. And then, according to Robert Lee Willie, Joe Vaccaro had stabbed Faith repeatedly in the chest and throat— "he just cut her throat, and he just started jugging her in the throat with it, man. Just jugging her, I mean jugging her." And the jury heard how Robert Lee Willie, the alleged ultimate bystander, had in his own words merely held her hands and told her to behave.

BOTH SIDES REST

As the tape ended, the faces of each of the jurors registered the shock and revulsion they now felt for the skinny blonde-haired man sitting just a few feet away from them. Herb could probably have rested his case at this point, but he decided to recall to the stand Dr. Paul McGarry, the pathologist who had performed the autopsy on Faith's body.

"Dr. McGarry," Herb began. "I want to ask you a hypothetical question. Assume that an eighteen-year-old female were to be stabbed in the throat area right around here ten or twelve times with a rather large knife. In your expert medical opinion, how long would it take for that person to die?"

"I would expect under those circumstances for the large arteries and veins in the neck to be penetrated and for death to occur in two or three minutes or so."

"How long can a person with those kinds of wounds continue to struggle or put up a forcible defense to such trauma?" Herb asked.

"Probably for a minute or two."

"Has it ever been your expert experience to find that type of tear in the vaginal wall, and it was not involved with a forcible rape of some type?"

"No, sir. There is not. I have not seen this kind of laceration in the vagina of a person who has not been raped."

"Has it ever been your experience to find that type of laceration in the vagina of a woman who had consensual sexual intercourse, in other words, consented to sexual intercourse with a man?"

114

"No, sir."

With that, the State rested its case.

With the jury out of the courtroom, Austin McElroy said, "I would like the record to reflect that I have discussed with Mr. Willie his testifying as a witness in his own behalf, and Mr. Willie has told me that he does not wish to do so, and I would ask Mr. Willie to affirm that at this time."

Willie said simply, "Right."

"There was also discussed the possibility of calling Joseph Vaccaro as a witness, and Mr. Willie has informed me that he does not wish to call Mr. Vaccaro as a witness, and I would ask Mr. Willie to affirm that."

Again, he simply said, "Right."

The jury was brought back in to the courtroom. Judge Crain said, "I believe the State has rested, Mr. McElroy."

"Yes, at this time the defendant, Robert Lee Willie, rests."

And so, with that simple statement, the trial was over except for the final arguments and the deliberations of the jury.

Judge Crain recessed the jury until the next morning when the final arguments would be given.

Driver's license photos of Robert Lee Willie and Joe Vaccaro.

St. Tammany Parish jail mug shot of Robert Lee Willie.

St. Tammany Parish jail mug shot of Joe Vaccaro.

The Lakefront Disco.

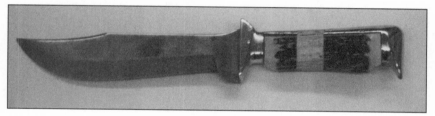

The murder weapon.

Faith Hathaway's grave. The teddy bear monument marks the grave of Baby Hope whose body was found on the shore of Lake Pontchartrain and buried next to Faith.

Judge Hillary J. Crain, who presided over the trial of Robert Lee Willie.

Reggie Simmons, who defended Joe Vaccaro.

District Attorney Marion Farmer.

Assistant District Attorney Herb Alexander, who prosecuted Robert Lee Willie in his first trial.

Assistant District Attorney Bill Alford,
who prosecuted Joe Vaccaro and Robert
Lee Willie in his second sentencing trial.

Willie and Vaccaro on their way out of court during the trials for the murder of Faith Hathaway. (*The Advocate*/Charles Gerald)

Robert Lee Willie in Cell Number 1, Death Row, Louisiana State Penitentiary at Angola. (*The State-Times*/Stan Alost)

Willie appearing before the Board of Pardons six weeks before his execution. (*The Advocate*/Gary Hunter)

Faith and her mother, Elizabeth Harvey.

Faith Hathaway as a young girl.

Faith in elementary school.

Faith in her senior class photo.

Faith on graduation night with Sergeant Farris, her Army
recruiter.

Faith with her mother, Elizabeth Harvey, and her grandfather,
Clarence Trawick.

Photos taken at the murder scene in Fricke's Cave, showing the position of Faith's body.

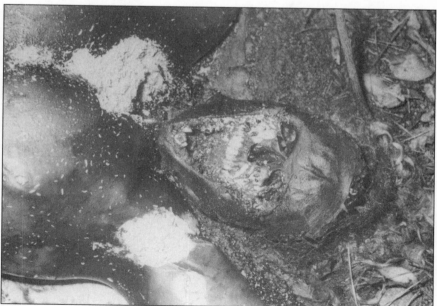

The infestation of maggots helped determine Faith's date of death. Also, note the "chalk line" they form around the body, further evidencing that Faith's body was not moved after her death.

Mike Varnado and Elizabeth Harvey on the riverfront in Madisonville where Debbie and Mark were kidnapped at gunpoint by Robert Lee Willie and Joe Vaccaro.

The Closing Arguments and a Verdict

The next morning, Thursday, October 23, Judge Crain convened court around 9:00 A.M. Before the jury was brought into the courtroom, Judge Crain asked Austin McElroy if he would like to make a motion before they began.

Austin McElroy accepted Judge Crain's invitation and moved for a mistrial based on an alleged violation of law by the District Attorney's Office—failing to turn over allegedly exculpatory material to the defense. The exculpatory evidence? A mysterious handwritten note allegedly found at Fricke's Cave the day before I found Faith's body. The note was written on the back of some type of receipt, and it read simply, "You never find her."

Judge Crain denied the motion for a mistrial, but said that he would inspect the note and consider it on a motion for a new trial. The jury was ushered into the courtroom by the bailiff and Herb Alexander began his closing argument.

He first thanked the jury for its service and he complimented them, saying that "I've been doing this for a long time, and this has been one of the most attentive juries that I have ever seen."

Herb Alexander then outlined the testimony of the witnesses presented, taking them in chronological order, building a compelling case for Robert Willie's guilt of the murder of Faith Hathaway. Herb was colloquial with the jury, talking with them like he was talking to each of them personally across the dining room table. He didn't use fancy words or lots of legalese. While holding the knife that had been introduced and which the State alleged to be the murder weapon, he said, "It's a mean-looking critter, ain't it?"

He used the evidence to great effect. He held up the shirt that had been torn off Faith, pointing out that it was found on the right-hand side of the highway running from Fricke's Cave to Covington. Herb argued that it had been thrown from the passenger side of the car, and that, according to Willie's own confession, he had been the passenger in the car, and Joe Vaccaro had been the one who was driving. "I passed that around to you all, and I am sure you took a good look at it, and I feel relatively sure that you noticed that there's not a button on it, and that there are some rather large tears where the buttons used to be. It's as though button, cloth, and all were ripped out. The tie on it is partly torn loose on one side. The sleeve is torn on one side and on the other side, as though that shirt had been ripped off of someone."

After going through a summary of the witnesses who had testified, Herb next went through Willie's confession, picking out parts of it and making cogent arguments about that particular section of the confession. For example, "Ladies and gentlemen of the jury, Joe Vaccaro might be capable of a lot of things, but he's not capable of driving a Ford Fairlane automobile and blindfolding somebody at the same time. There is no way in the world Joe Vaccaro could have driven that car and blindfolded Faith Hathaway at the same time. And then all of a sudden, Willie testifies he's just sitting in the car looking out the window, not paying any attention to anything that's going on."

After Herb finished and sat down, Austin McElroy rose to argue for his client, Robert Willie. He first thanked the jury for their service. "I also wish to thank you for your attention. You have had to suffer a hardship three nights, not being able to see your families, being locked alone in a room with no television, and this has been an especially hard time for the men because there was a football game and the World Series on television."

He said, "Now if I stood up here today and told you that Faith Hathaway wasn't killed and that Robert Willie had nothing to do with it, you would think I was a fool. I'm not going to do that. Robert Willie's statement shows that he was there, and there is more than enough evidence to show that Faith Hathaway was killed. We know that on the morning of May 28 of this year, Faith Hathaway was killed, and that Robert Willie was there. We also know that Joseph Vaccaro is the man who cut Faith Hathaway's throat. We know Robert Willie was involved, but what exactly was his involvement?"

Austin argued that Willie's involvement was minimal, and thus, he should not be convicted of first-degree murder. He said, "Totally and unexpectedly, Joseph Vaccaro pulls out the knife that Eddie Sharp had given to him and starts cutting Faith Hathaway. Robert Willie was under the influence of drugs. You or I probably would have punched or even killed Joe Vaccaro at that point. But then you and I are not under the influence of drugs. Robert Willie didn't kill Faith Hathaway. Robert Willie didn't know that Joseph Vaccaro was going to kill Faith Hathaway. He acted in a manner that offends everybody, but he's not guilty of murdering Faith Hathaway. To find Robert Lee Willie guilty, you have to find that he had the specific intent to kill. I submit to you based on the evidence you cannot find that. Thank you."

When Herb rose again to offer the last argument to the jury on rebuttal, he moved quickly to address the last point made by Austin McElroy—that Robert Willie was too drugged out to know what he was doing. "Let's get rid of this business about Robert Lee Willie being full of Valiums, full of LSD, full of beer. Number one, nobody poured any beer down his throat, nobody poured any Valiums down his throat, and nobody poured any LSD down his throat. Number two, would a man who is so high on beer, Valiums and LSD that he doesn't know what he's doing and who can't form the specific intent to participate in the murder of a eighteen-year-old girl be able to remember what you heard in this twelve-page typewritten document? Could he remember the facts? Could he remember what time they picked her up? Could he remember her first name? Could he remember that Joe blind-folded her by Barker's Store? Could he remember that they came up Lee Road and cut across to Folsom and then went on up to Fricke's Cave? Could he remember that they went to the Corner Pack, or whatever the name of that store is on the Hill in Covington?"

Herb also focused the jury's attention on the length of time that Faith was with Willie and Vaccaro before she was killed. Of course, it seems likely that Willie and Vaccaro abducted Faith before 2:30 A.M., but even if Willie's testimony that Faith was picked up at 4:30 is accepted, she was with them for five hours before she was killed. "Why did it take from 4:30 in the morning, Robert Lee Willie's words, to between 9:00 and 10:00 in the morning before they killed her?" Herb asked. "Why did it take five hours when it was a forty-five minute drive? What do you think they did to that girl for five hours? They tore her up inside raping her is what they did, and after they finished raping her and they had all they wanted, they took her naked and blind-folded down into Fricke's Cave."

Before Herb closed his argument, he made a point that must have struck like a bolt of lightning in the minds of the jurors. Willie would be guilty of first-degree murder even if he were not the one who wielded the knife if he assisted in her killing, but Herb argued that Willie's own words showed that he was the one who actually had stabbed Faith. "You remember when I got the two men to lie down in the courtroom and demonstrate for you how the girl's body was found, with her hands up stretched over her head, her knees bent, and her feet down on the ground and her legs up like this," Herb said. "If Robert Lee Willie was in front of her, to be able to hold her hands, he would have to reach all the way across the top of her, ladies and gentlemen, and he'd have gotten in the way of Joe Vaccaro in back of her gouging that knife ten or twelve times in her throat and upper chest area, wouldn't he have?"

Herb completed his closing argument. "We do know not only

beyond a reasonable doubt, but beyond any doubt that Robert Willie is guilty of first-degree murder. First-degree murder. That is the verdict that we ask you to return in this proceeding. Thank you."

Judge Crain began to instruct the jury on the law, explaining to them all the intricacies of the law that would have to be applied to the facts—things like the defendant is presumed to be innocent until each element of the crime necessary to constitute his guilt is proven beyond a reasonable doubt. After the judge instructed the jurors, he excused the two alternates. The jury retired to deliberate on the fate of Robert Willie at 10:45 A.M. All told, the arguments of the State and the defense and the instructions to the jury had taken about two hours.

The jury left the courtroom and moved in a group, escorted by the bailiff, to the jury deliberation room. It did not take long for them to return a verdict. Almost exactly an hour later, at 11:45 A.M., the jury notified the bailiff that they had reached a verdict, and they were escorted back into the courtroom.

Judge Crain waited for the jury to be seated in the box. He then turned to the jury and asked, "Have you reached a verdict?"

Vernon Carr, the foreman of the jury, selected by his fellow jurors, rose and said, "We sure have."

Judge Crain said, "Will you come forward, please, sir, and hand me your verdict?"

Vernon Carr handed the verdict, written on a sheet of paper to the judge. Judge Crain looked at the verdict and handed it to the clerk. "The clerk will read the verdict."

The clerk rose and read the verdict. "We, the jury, find the defendant guilty of first-degree murder."

Austin McElroy rose and asked the judge to poll the jury—that is, ask each of the twelve jurors if the verdict of guilty was his or her own individual verdict.

"Will you just say that is your verdict when the clerk of court calls your name one by one so that we can poll and make sure the required number has made a verdict?"

One by one until all twelve jurors had their chance to respond, they all either answered yes, yes ma'am, or nodded.

After the jury had been polled, Judge Crain again addressed them.

"Ladies and gentlemen, since there is a verdict of guilty as charged in this case of first-degree murder, we will now have to go into the second phase of the trial, which is the sentencing hearing." Before they began, Judge Crain recessed for lunch. He was intent on keeping things moving, however. It was right around noon, and he recessed court only until 1:00 P.M.

A SENTENCE OF DEATH

After lunch, the jury returned and the sentencing phase of Robert Lee Willie's trial began. The State's first witness was Charles H. Parker.

Herb's first question seemingly was an innocuous one, "Where do you live, Mr. Parker?"

The answer was equally innocuous. "I live in New Orleans, Louisiana."

Herb Alexander's next question, however, showed that Charles Parker was no ordinary citizen, living in a quiet neighborhood some place in the Crescent City. "In what institution are you housed?"

"I cannot answer that right now, sir."

"Why not?"

"It's for security reasons."

Now, the jury was really interested. Herb continued. "Are you in a penal institution down there?"

"Yes."

"Are you housed in the same penal institution in New Orleans that Robert Lee Willie is housed in?"

"No, I'm not."

"Were you ever housed in the same one with him?"

"Yes, I was, from around September 9 up until last week."

Charles Parker continued by recounting how he had met Robert Lee Willie on the Quad, which was a section in the prison where all the inmates are housed. Upon questioning by Herb, he admitted that he had been convicted of one felony, destruction of junk mail. He was presently being held on thirteen counts of making false claims against the U.S. government. He acknowledged that the U.S. attorney had made a plea bargain with him to drop eleven of the counts if he would testify against Robert Lee Willie. He had already pled guilty to two counts, and although he had not yet been sentenced, he faced a maximum penalty of ten years and a fine of $10,000. He testified that he had not been promised a suspended sentence.

Charles H. Parker said that on Saturday, September 27, he asked Willie about Faith Hathaway. Willie said that he had had sex with Faith two or three times, and Vaccaro had had sex with her once. Willie also said that he was the one who had cut Faith's throat. He also said that Vaccaro urinated in her face, as she lay dying or dead. Willie laughed as he told Parker this.

Although Charles Parker was not allowed to testify concerning everything that Willie had told him on the Quad in the New Orleans prison where they were both held, Parker had told authorities that Willie was convinced that he would never have to answer for his convictions in state court because he was already serving multiple life sentences imposed by a federal court for the kidnapping of Mark Brewster and Debbie Cuevas. To Willie, it was unimportant whether or not he received the death penalty. He told Parker, "I'm doing this Fed time and will be out on the streets before you are, Check Casher. I got this haircut, and this has changed my looks. I'm going to beat this murder case."

Willie also had told Parker that he wanted to kill Tommy Holden and several of the law enforcement officers who had been instrumental in his arrest. When asked how he planned to kill them, he said, "Like Jack the Ripper. I'll cut their throats so they'll never talk again. They don't know how dangerous it is with their jobs. I wouldn't want a job where I had to look over my shoulder, down the street, and at every red light. That kills you slowly. Let everybody be his own law. I'm like Son of Sam." He threatened to kill Parker if he "ratted" on him. "My people are close to the Mafia," he said.

The jury never heard these threats of Robert Lee Willie. Instead, after Parker had testified that Willie had bragged about cutting Faith's throat and that Vaccaro had urinated in her face as she lay dying, Herb tendered the witness to the defense. Austin began his cross-examination.

His first question was right to the point. "Do you know what a snitch is?"

When Parker admitted that he did, Austin asked, "Isn't it a fact that while you were in the Community Correctional Center that you were known as a snitch and no one would talk to you?"

Parker said, "That there is a lie."

After an FBI special agent from Washington testified that human blood had been found on the knife that Willie and Vaccaro had had, the State rested its case. It was now up to Austin McElroy to do what he could to save Willie's life. "The defense calls Elizabeth Oalman," he said.

Elizabeth Oalman, Robert Lee Willie's mother, walked slowly to the witness stand, her eyes cast down, avoiding the stare of her son as she sat at the defense table. After being sworn in, Elizabeth Oalman began by telling the jury that John Willie, Robert's father, was himself an inmate in Angola. She also testified that John Willie had not been around much when Robert was growing up. "He hardly ever asked about Robert. He hardly ever seen Robert. Robert and I stayed with my mother and father up until I married the second time," she said.

Elizabeth Oalman told the jury that she became aware that Robert was using drugs and drinking after he left home when he was about sixteen. She said that he drank very heavily at times. Austin asked her if Willie had ever been violent. She said, "No, not really." She paused, perhaps thinking of the time when Willie and another boy beat their victim senseless with a broomstick. "Well, when he was drinking. He wasn't really around me that much."

"Do you love your son?" Austin asked.

"I love my son dearly," she said.

Herb Alexander had no questions for Mrs. Oalman. As she passed by her son, she began to cry. Robert Willie looked up at his mother and said, "Oh, dry it up. I've got ninety years. Don't worry about it."

The next defense witness was Hazel Taylor, Robert Willie's aunt. She testified that Robert had had a rough life since he was about five years old. "He was raised from one place to another. He's really never had no home. Everywhere he has put his leg down, that was home."

Mrs. Taylor said that Willie had stayed with her, his mother and with his grandmother. She also testified that Robert had used LSD and had been a drinker. As Elizabeth Oalman had said, Willie's aunt testified that Willie "wasn't a violent person."

"Do you love Robert Lee Willie?" Austin asked.

"Yes, I do," she said.

Again, Herb had no questions. After a fifteen-minute recess, the defense rested.

Marion Farmer, the Washington Parish District Attorney, rose to give the closing argument for the state.

He commented that to his knowledge this was the first time in the one hundred fifty years that Washington Parish had existed that two jury trials had been going on at one time in the same courthouse. He also commented on the fact that Faith Hathaway had been about to go into the Army. "I think that's kind of interesting and unique these days. Just recently we all know what has happened with the draft registration. Some of the young men did not even want to register for the draft, and here we have a young lady who takes it upon herself to serve her country."

As Marion walked slowly in front of the jury box, all eyes were on him. "It appears obvious that by his deliberate actions Mr. Willie has forfeited and given up his right to exist on this earth as a human being like the rest of us," Marion said. "I think you probably noticed during the playing of the tape, a very emotional moment for all of us, you could hear a pin drop in this court-room. You probably noticed he showed no emotion whatsoever. He sat there as his voice detailed exactly how this horrible, hideous crime was committed, never flinched, never did any-thing but smirk a few times, never did one thing, had no emotion whatsoever. I think it's obvious that he had no remorse at all."

Marion closed by saying, "I think if there ever was or ever will be a death penalty case, this is that case. We ask you to return a penalty of death in this case. Thank you."

Austin stood and walked to the front of the jury box. He looked at each of the jurors one by one, before making a con-fession himself. "I will be quite frank with you. This is the first time in my life I've ever had to argue for someone else's life, and it scares the hell out of me because I know I'm not going to say everything I should say, because I'm scared."

He next launched into an attack on Charles Parker, the inmate in New Orleans who had testified that he had received a jailhouse confession from Willie. He argued that the only reason Parker testified as he did was to help himself in his fraud case in federal court. He argued that Parker had gotten details from newspaper accounts.

Austin argued that a life sentence-"your freedom taken away from you, going where you're told to go, eating when you're told to eat, sleeping when you're told to sleep, getting up when you're told to get up, everything you do and the greater major-ity of that time spent behind bars"-was proper punishment for Willie. He said that the death penalty is revenge and that revenge should be reserved to God, not man. He also argued that putting Willie to death would not bring Faith back.

Austin also focused the jury's attention on the fact that both Willie's mother and his aunt loved him. "In spite of what he has done, his mother and aunt still love him, so we know that there are at least two people on this earth who care for Robert Willie, and when you consider what sentence to impose, consider what the maximum sentence would do to those two people."

After Austin concluded his closing argument, Herb Alexander rose to make the final argument to the jury. As Austin McElroy had done, he too made a confession. "This is a first for me, this is the first time I've ever stood before a jury and asked them to take a man's life."

Herb made an impassioned argument for the death penalty. In closing, he addressed Austin's argument that Willie would serve the rest of his life in prison if he were given a life sentence. "The statute does say no probation, no parole, no suspension of sentence, but have you ever heard of a pardon or commutation? Those are two things that are given to the governor of the State of Louisiana in the Constitution of the State of Louisiana and it can't be taken away by statute. As a result, the governor, whoever the governor is eight, ten, twelve years from now, fifteen years from now, twenty years from now, can take it upon himself to let Robert Lee Willie back out onto the streets and back out into society because that governor more than likely will not know the facts of this case. So don't think that life really ever means life, because it doesn't."

Herb continued. "The other thing is a lot of times people would like to let jurors think the buck stops with you. Ladies and gentlemen of the jury, every word that has been said during the course of this trial, every piece of evidence that has been entered into the record during the course of this trial, all the motions that were filed and heard prior to this trial, and everything will more than likely be reviewed by every appeals court in this state, including the Supreme Court of this state. It has to go to them, as a matter of fact, by law, and once that's over, then the federal appeal begins, both in the district courts, the federal district courts, the federal appellate courts, and the Supreme Court of the United States of America, before anybody is put in the chair. So the buck really don't stop with you. The buck starts with you. So what I'm asking you to do is start the buck rolling."

Herb thanked the jury and sat down.

After the judge instructed the jury on the law, the jury retired to deliberate at 3:00 P.M. At 3:50 P.M., word was sent to Judge Crain that the jury had reached a verdict. The courtroom was silent as the members of the jury filed back into the jury box.

The sentence was handed to the clerk who handed it to Judge Crain. He read it and then handed it back to the clerk.

"The defendant will please rise," Judge Crain said. All of the lawyers stood. Robert Lee Willie, who a moment before had been slouching and smirking at the jury, also stood up.

"The clerk will please read the verdict," Judge Crain said.

"In the Matter of the State of Louisiana versus Robert Lee Willie," the clerk began, saying all of the words that had to be said before the actual verdict was announced. At the moment of truth, the clerk paused for an instant. The next word would be either life or death.

As the Harveys sat tensely waiting on the front row, the clerk continued.

"Death."

A Second Guilty Verdict

While the trial of Robert Lee Willie was proceeding in the basement courtroom, Joe Vaccaro's murder trial was going on at the same time in an upstairs courtroom. Much of the testimony was the same as that in Willie's trial, although Bill Alford was able to call Debbie Cuevas to testify since she had had a personal conversation with Joe Vaccaro about Faith Hathaway. I remember running back and forth between the two courtrooms, and it was much the same for many of the other witnesses.

After both the State and the defense had rested their cases, Bill Alford made an impassioned closing argument. He described how Faith's body provided a roadmap for the jury to see in determining the guilt of Vaccaro.

"You know," Bill said, "there is an old saying that dead men tell no tales, but in this case, you have a case where Faith Hathaway is screaming out to you, her body is screaming to you, and it is telling you things. It is telling you things that you can't ignore. What is it telling you? You heard the evidence. It is telling you that she was nude. It is telling you that her throat was cut, and what does that mean? Do you recall what Dr. McGarry told you about the throat cut? That this would not be immediate death. That this would be painful. That this would mean gasping for breath. What else does she tell you? Her right hand is cut. This means she is trying to fight. She is trying to defend herself, to save her life. She is nude. Her legs were as wide apart as they could be. What is that body telling you? That body is telling you somebody was between my legs and somebody was holding my hands and I was fighting and I didn't have any clothes on and they cut my throat. Her body is telling you that just as plain as if this girl could be here today on that witness stand and speak to you, just that plain."

After Tom Ford made a closing argument for the defense and Bill made his rebuttal argument, Judge James instructed the jury. The jury retired to deliberate at 4:42 p.m.

The jury returned with a verdict at 6:25 p.m. The foreman of the jury handed the verdict to the bailiff who handed it up to Judge James. Judge James looked at the verdict and handed it to the clerk to read. "State of Louisiana versus Joseph Vaccaro, Number 35,802, Twenty-Second Judicial District Court, Parish of Washington, State of Louisiana. Verdict: We, the jury, find the defendant guilty."

EVIDENCE FOR LIFE, EVIDENCE FOR DEATH

After some sparring between the lawyers over certain evidence to be introduced during the sentencing phase of Vaccaro's trial, the jury was then brought into the courtroom, and Bill began his opening statement. He outlined that the jury would have two verdicts to choose from: death or life imprisonment at hard labor without benefit of parole, probation or suspension of sentence.

Reggie Simmons, Vaccaro's defense attorney, got up and gave his opening statement. He mentioned that Vaccaro had suffered from mental or emotional disturbances since his childhood, and that he was the type of person who would be easily influenced or dominated by others. He also noted that Vaccaro had a history of addiction to drugs and alcohol. "You will be shown that he is a man who is very unhappy with himself, a man who has attempted suicide by stabbing himself in the abdomen with a coat hanger."

Bill Alford called two witnesses in support of the death penalty for Vaccaro. One was the Assistant U.S. Attorney who had prosecuted Vaccaro for his part in the kidnapping of Debbie Cuevas and Mark Brewster. The other was Vaccaro's probation and parole officer. Both of these men testified as to Vaccaro's criminal history, a history that included kidnapping, auto theft, attempted theft, escape and burglary.

The first witness called by the defense was Katherine L. Daggy, Joe Vaccaro's mother.

"Has your son ever been committed to the Southeast Louisiana Hospital in Mandeville?" Reggie asked.

"Yes, he has. Twice." She also testified that he had been treated at the St. Tammany Mental Health Center.

"Mrs. Daggy, did your son ever have any difficulty sleeping?"

"Yes, he has always had difficulty sleeping, as a child."

"Do you know whether or not any prescription drugs were made available to him through a prescription for sleeping?"

"Valiums is all."

"When Joseph was a young boy, did he exhibit any problems learning in school?" Reggie asked.

"Yes, he was evaluated. He could not get no book learning at all in school."

"What grade in school was he when he was evaluated?"

"Fifth grade, fourth grade."

"Can he read and write now?"

"No, he cannot," she said.

"After you had taken him for evaluation, did they tell you whether or not he would probably be able to learn to read and write?"

"They said that he could not learn any kind of book learning, that he could learn mechanical—anything with his hands, enough to make a living, but no book learning."

"When did you and Mr. Vaccaro separate?"

"Joe was about thirteen."

"Have you and your son been able to get along with one another?"

"Yes, very well."

"Does he have problems meeting people?"

"No, he does not."

"Is it difficult for him to make friends?"

"No, he makes friends very easily."

"Did his father express any love for his son?"

"No, he did not."

"Did Mr. Vaccaro domineer or dominate his son?"

"Yes, he did."

"Mrs. Daggy, was he married at the age of seventeen?" Reggie asked.

"Yes, he was."

"How long did he remain married approximately?"

"I would say a year or two, his first marriage."

"After that period of time, did he divorce his first wife?"

"Yes."

"Did they have a child?"

"Yes, one boy."

"Is that child still living?"

"Yes, he is."

"Did he subsequently marry someone else?"

"Yes, he did."

"Does he have any children by his marriage to Bonnie, his second wife?"

"Yes."

Mrs. Daggy also testified that Joe had some half brothers or sisters and that they all loved one another. She also testified that her sister had been in a mental institution several times in Louisiana and in Texas—one time for two years. She also testified to her own problem with nerves, a condition that necessitated her taking Valiums, which Joe sometimes stole from her. She testified as to his drug addiction from the age of thirteen. She told a story of how he had once gotten his car stuck in the mud and threw bricks at the car, breaking the windows and beating the car up.

She testified that all his scrapes with the law occurred when he was on drugs or alcohol. She said that she had seen him have fits, "falling out spells from taking drugs."

She also testified that he was "easily influenced. He was easily led."

On cross-examination, Bill went right in on Vaccaro's mother. "Mrs. Daggy, what you seem to paint, correct me if I am wrong, is a picture of your son who since about thirteen years of age hasn't been very responsible, has he?"

She agreed and Bill continued. "He has failed at everything he has done, is that right?"

"No, I wouldn't say he failed at everything he has done. He succeeded in making a living for himself, working."

She said that Vaccaro had three children. Vaccaro's father had adopted Vaccaro's oldest son and was raising him.

She said that Vaccaro was a mechanic when he worked and wasn't in jail.

"Do you recall ever expressing, telling anybody that you were afraid of Joe Vaccaro," Bill asked.

"No."

"You don't remember ever telling the hospital that you were afraid of him?"

"No, I remember telling the hospital that I was afraid that he would hurt himself."

"You don't recall ever indicating any fear that he might hurt other people, too?"

"Well, possibly, yes."

"In the latter part of May, 1980, was Joe Vaccaro living with you?"

"He stayed at my house, between my house and my mother's house."

"Was he working?"

"He just did odd jobs."

"Was he supporting his kids?"

"Not to my knowledge."

Next, Reggie read a report into the record of Vaccaro's mental evaluation. It had a great deal of background information about Vaccaro, including that he had one daughter, who was age two. Also he had one younger half-brother and two younger half-sisters. The report noted that "treatment will include chemotherapy and group therapy to help the patient with impulse control." The date on the discharge report was January 10, 1977. At that time, he was living at Jim's Motel in Covington. His IQ was in the dull normal range. "Potentially, he could be of normal intelligence," the report noted. It added that Vaccaro "was brought in because of threatening to hurt himself and others, because of his severe rage attacks. He was a rather sickly looking white male with a spaced out look and very flat affect. It was felt at the time of admission that his diagnosis was schizophrenia, chronic undifferentiated type, drug abuse and possible psychomotor seizures. Diagnosis—antisocial personality. Drug abuse. Prognosis—poor. The patient has a history of violent temper and possibly some seizures."

After reading the evaluation into the record, Reggie rested for the defense. There was no rebuttal by the state and closing arguments began.

A Plea for Mercy

In his closing argument to the jury during the sentencing phase of Joe Vaccaro's trial, Bill Alford pointed back to a statement made by Reggie Simmons at the beginning of the trial, when he said, "If you return a sentence of life imprisonment, then Joe Vaccaro will leave jail in a box."

Bill said, "If I knew that that were true, I might not be up here arguing for the infliction of capital punishment. But I don't know that that is true and you don't know if that is true and there is no way that anybody is going to know that that is true. There is only one way to make sure that that man can't reap any more misery on innocent people."

Bill was rolling now. As he paced in front of the jury box, he recalled Vaccaro's criminal history. "Since 1971, he has been a criminal," he said. "He has been convicted of five felonies: two thefts, a burglary, two simple escapes. He has been convicted in federal court of two counts of kidnapping. How much do we have to endure? How much do we as a society have to endure? How much do we have to take? How much do we have to pay? Do we say to the Faith Hathaways of the world, 'Too bad. You're just going to have to keep paying. You're just going to have to keep paying.' And the Debbie Cuevases, 'You're just going to have to keep paying,' the Mark Brewsters, 'You're just going to have to keep paying.'"

Bill stopped and let this last argument sink in before launching his next attack. "His mother testified and I am at a loss really to think of what the defense hoped to gain by putting his mother on the stand and by reading his psychiatric record into the record, because what kind of picture does it paint? What kind of person is Joe Vaccaro? Is he worth for one moment a Faith Hathaway? For one moment, a girl that was trying to do something with her life? A girl that had hopes for the future? She wasn't a dope addict, she hadn't been a poor student."

Bill was reaching the climax of his argument. "It is not easy to say death," he said. "I know that it is not easy, but if you don't, if you don't and somebody else dies, another Faith Hathaway, or somebody else, where does the responsibility lie? What does that person say? My God, why did you give him a chance? What does that mother say or what does that father say? Why did you give him a chance to do that again? You knew what he was. Why did you do it? Please don't do it, ladies and gentlemen. We ask that you return a verdict of death in the electric chair. Thank you."

Bill Alford's closing argument for death ran just five pages in the transcript, not much more than a thousand words. Bill's closing argument took between five and ten minutes to deliver.

Reggie Simmons got up now and began his appeal to save Joe Vaccaro from the electric chair. His argument would take fifty-two pages in the final transcript. He spoke to the jury for between an hour and an hour and a half.

He told the jury that a life sentence in this case meant a life sentence. "It means when you leave, you will leave the penitentiary with your feet pointed to the Lord in a box. You are as dead as a hammer. You never leave the penitentiary as long as you breathe. You die in the penitentiary."

Reggie continued. "Let me tell you something. The State is asking you to kill somebody. We are in a trial here today because somebody was killed, and that man sitting right there is asking you to kill someone else." And he pointed at Bill Alford.

Reggie Simmons was and is a devout Christian. It is perhaps not surprising, therefore, that he focused a large part of his closing argument on the Bible. He quoted Jesus's admonition to turn the other cheek and to love your enemies and bless those who curse you. He recounted the story of the woman caught in the act of adultery who was brought before Jesus. Reggie reminded the jury that Jesus told the accusers "let he who is without sin, let him cast the first stone."

Reggie stood before the jury and looked each of them directly in the eye. "Which among you is more able than Jesus to judge Joe Vaccaro? If Jesus gives life, who among you is qualified to decree death?" Reggie asked.

Reggie also recounted the story of Cain killing his brother, Abel. He noted that God did not impose the death sentence on Cain, but banished him from his homeland. "Do any of you know any worse place to be in the world than in prison?" Reggie asked. "Sometimes if you really want to hurt somebody, death is not the worse way, it is not the worst thing you can do to them. God didn't kill Cain. He was hoping for death. God chose to let Cain live with whatever he had done. Is not the mark of Cain upon Joseph Vaccaro?"

Reggie also recounted a personal story, one based on his own family history. "There was a man named Ansel," he said. "He lived in Franklinton and he had a friend. Let's call him Robert. Ansel and Robert were the best of friends. They did everything they could together. They went fishing. They had good times together. They went on dates together.

"One night they went out and they got to drinking and they were having a lot of fun and they both got drunk and the next morning Ansel woke up in a jail cell. He said, 'Hey, jailer, what am I doing in this jail cell? I ain't never been in jail in my life.'

"The jailer said, 'Ansel, you know why you are in this jail cell.'

"He said, 'I don't know anything. Where is Robert?'

"The jailer said, 'You killed Robert last night.'

"And Ansel pled guilty to manslaughter. He went to prison. While he was in prison, he studied law. When he got out of prison, he moved to Napoleonville. He became a practicing attorney after passing the bar. He became the mayor of that town and, in late 1950, my uncle Ansel was killed in a car wreck."

At this point, the transcript notes that Reggie became emotional. He was crying and the jury was becoming emotional as well. Women were wiping their eyes. One was near tears.

"My cousin, Ansel Junior—they call him Buster—is still practicing law in Napoleonville. There was a man who had done something wrong, but he was able to come out of it all right. I don't know what Joe Vaccaro will do with a chance, if you give it to him. I submit to you though-don't we owe it to him? Don't we owe it to ourselves to give him a chance?"

In closing, Reggie returned to the dominant theme of his closing argument. "Let me ask you one more question. If Jesus Christ were on this jury tonight, would you have any doubt whatsoever what his verdict would be? What would Jesus do? Do you think he would vote for death? I don't think so. I submit to you that the right thing to do in this case is to let Joseph Vaccaro's death be a matter between God and him."

The court took a break and then Bill Alford began his rebuttal argument.

He began by saying that he also went to church and believed in God and Jesus, but he didn't believe in using religion to try and influence a jury.

"Down in those dark, damp woods," Bill said, "did Joe Vaccaro and Robert Willie submit Faith Hathaway's fate to twelve citizens? Did they appoint her a lawyer? Did they advise her of her rights? They were the judge and the jury and they did it."

When Bill finished his argument, Judge James charged the jury on the law, and they retired to deliberate.

The time was 11:33 p.m. The jury returned with their verdict at 1:10 a.m.

Judge James asked the jury if they had reached a verdict. The jury foreman said, "Your Honor, we are unable to reach a unanimous verdict." The vote was eleven to one in favor of the death penalty. One juror had held out against the death penalty and, in effect, had saved Vaccaro's life.

Judge James asked, "Do you feel that by any further deliberation you could reach a verdict or do you feel that you are hopelessly deadlocked?"

The foreman said, "Your Honor, my personal opinion is that we are deadlocked."

Judge James asked, "Does the balance of the jury feel essentially the same way?"

The jurors all said yes and shook their hands in the affirmative.

Because the jury had failed to reach a verdict, under law, Judge James was required to and did impose a sentence of life without the benefit of probation, parole or suspension of sentence on Joe Vaccaro.

THE LEGAL MACHINERY
GRINDS ON

On November 10, 1980, about a month after the trials of Willie and Vaccaro for the murder of Faith Hathaway, Willie and Vaccaro were tried for three counts of rape of Debbie Cuevas. Because of the intense media attention in the case, Judge John S. Covington moved the trial from Covington, Louisiana, to Baton Rouge.

The first day of the trial was consumed with the selection of the jury. At the end of the day, the jury had finally been selected and the prosecution had made its opening statement. After the defense waived its opening statement, court was adjourned for the day.

After a full day off, the trial resumed on November 12 in the morning and ran until late afternoon. Debbie Cuevas was forced during the three days of trial to relive and to testify in open court about the horrors she had lived through at the hands of Robert Lee Willie and Joe Vaccaro. Willie smirked all the way through the trial as the State put on its proof against him and Vaccaro. At one point, Willie even blew Debbie a kiss.

At one point during the trial, Mark Brewster was called by the prosecution to stand in the doorway of the courtroom so that he could be identified by Bruce Hostetter, an investigator for the St. Tammany District Attorney's Office and Stanley Fant, an investigator with the Alabama Department of Public Safety, both of whom were in the group who had found Mark in the woods. At the time of the trial, Mark had regained his ability to walk with difficulty, but his right arm dangled loose at his side.

When Willie saw Mark, he drew his finger across his own throat and said, "Looking good." The jury gasped at Willie's total lack of remorse.

After the state had presented its proof, Willie and Vaccaro surprised everyone by changing their pleas from not guilty to guilty. They said that since the State was trying to "do it" to them, they wanted to make the State spend the money to try them. As they left the courtroom, Willie waved at Judge Covington and said, "See ya later, Cap."

A little over eighteen months later, on January 25, 1982, the Louisiana Supreme Court ruled that Herb's closing argument in Robert Lee Willie's trial was improper in two respects. The first improper argument was the one that asked the jury to impose death on Willie so that a governor would not later pardon him or commute his sentence. The second improper argument was the one that the buck did not stop with the jury, but that it merely started with them. Because of these two arguments that Herb had made to the jury, the Court said that there was a "reasonable possibility that the death sentence was imposed under the influence of passion, prejudice or arbitrary factors." As a result, the Court ordered that Willie receive a new sentencing hearing. In effect, Willie would have a second chance to avoid the electric chair.

In addition, the Court remanded the case back to Judge Crain's court for him to determine if the note that had been found in Fricke's Cave that read, "You never find her," would have made any difference on the issue of guilt or innocence if the defense had known about the note prior to trial and had been able to use it in the defense of Willie. If Judge Crain determined that the note might have made a difference to the jury in deciding Willie's guilt or innocence, Willie would not merely get a second chance to avoid the electric chair—he would get a new trial and another chance to avoid all responsibility for the murder of Faith Hathaway.

THE MYSTERIOUS NOTE

On June 28, 1982, just a month past the two-year anniversary of the murder of Faith Hathaway and about twenty months after Robert Willie had been convicted of her murder and had been sentenced to death, he walked once again into a courtroom in Franklinton, Louisiana. As before, Austin McElroy and Tom Ford represented Willie. District Attorney Marion Farmer assigned Bill Alford, who had prosecuted Joe Vaccaro at trial, to handle the State's case against Willie. Judge Hillary J. Crain again presided over the proceedings.

All that the defense was able to show with respect to the note was that the note had been found at the base of the steep slope in Fricke's Cave on Tuesday, June 3, the day before I discovered Faith's body, that none of the individuals who had found it had written the note or knew who had or where it had come from, and that it had not been fingerprinted because it had been handled so completely by everyone who had come into contact with it. Austin had wanted to question each of the original jurors as to whether the note would have made a difference to them in deciding Willie's guilt or innocence. Austin had actually subpoenaed all of the original jurors, so that they were waiting in the hallway. Judge Crain would have none of this, however. The original jurors were told they could go home.

Bill Alford's first witness was from the Louisiana State Police. She testified that no fingerprints could be identified on the note. I was called as the next witness.

Bill Alford first got the introductory questions out of the way—who I was, that I worked for the District Attorney's Office, and that I was involved in the investigation of the murder of Faith Hathaway.

Bill finally showed me the actual note that had been marked as an exhibit. "I would ask you if you recall ever having seen that actual piece of paper?"

I had not, never.

Next, I was asked if I had ever seen a copy of the note. I had, of course. I told everyone where—in the District Attorney's case file.

Bill Alford asked incredulously, "There is a copy of that note in the case file?"

I calmly and strongly said yes.

"Did you have an occasion to go to Texarkana, Arkansas, and interview one Robert Willie?"

"Yes, sir. I did."

"And when you interviewed Robert Willie, did you inquire of him as to whether or not he had written a note?"

"Yes, sir."

"And did he say he had written a note?"

"He denied writing a note."

"Did you ask him whether or not Joe Vaccaro had written a note?"

"I asked him did anybody write a note he was aware of."

"And what was his response?

"He said 'No note.'"

"Did he admit his involvement in the death of Faith Hathaway?"

"Yes, sir."

"But he said that neither he nor Joe Vaccaro wrote a note?"

"No note."

"In the course of your investigation, were you able to determine as best you could whether or not Joe Vaccaro could write?"

"Could not, is my understanding."

"Now after the arrest and during the months before the trial, did you ever have occasion to speak with the defense attorney, Mr. Austin McElroy, concerning the facts and circumstances involved in the Robert Willie case?"

"I can't remember specifically talking to Mr. Austin McElroy, but I do know that I talked to Sal Liberto and Reggie Simmons, and there were at least three or four defense attorneys there on several occasions and everything in the case was discussed."

"And the note was discussed many times prior to trial?"

"Certainly."

"And was there any effort on your part or on anyone else's part to keep the note a secret?"

"No, sir."

"Is the note referred to in the statement given by Robert Willie?"

"Yes, sir."

"Do you have direct knowledge of the fact that defense counsel was given a copy of that statement?"

"Yes, sir."

"Were the attorneys for the defendant ever allowed to review the D.A.'s file?"

"The whole complete file, pictures and everything."

"And was there a copy of the note in the file?"

"Yes, sir. Several copies of the note."

"Did you feel, sir, that the note had any significance insofar as the death of Faith Hathaway?"

"No, sir."

Bill Alford sat down after making clear that numerous people had been in the Cave since Faith's things had been found there on Sunday, June 1. Austin McElroy stalked toward me, clearly upset with the turn of events. I continued to be a thorn in his side, but as always, I was just telling the truth. His client, Robert Willie, had just dug his own grave a little too deep.

"Mr. Varnado, did you or any member of your staff cause an investigation to be made into the source of that note?"

"Yes, sir. I did."

"And what type of investigation did you do?"

"Well, after I asked Mr. Willie about the note, that's as far as I went into it since he denied it."

"Did you ever attempt to have the handwriting analyzed?"

"No, sir."

"Did you ever attempt to find the source of the receipt itself that is on the reverse side of that note?"

"No, sir."

"Did you ever ask Joe Vaccaro if he wrote the note?"

"I don't remember asking him. I feel certain that I did, but I don't remember."

"Now you said you told Sal Liberto about the existence of this note. Do you know who in this case Sal Liberto represented?"

"No, but I remember Sal being there."

"And you remember telling Mr. Simmons about the existence of the note?"

"Yes, sir."

"How about Mr. Ford?"

"Seems like Mr. Ford was there as well."

"But you don't remember telling me about it?"

"I don't remember your being there, Mr. McElroy. I took it that you were."

"I have no further questions."

The next witness to be called by Bill Alford was Herb Alexander, the lawyer who prosecuted Robert Willie at trial.

"Mr. Alexander, during the course of the pretrial preparation, did you have numerous conferences and meetings with the defense attorneys in the case?"

"Yes, I did."

"Was there ever any discussion of a note?"

"Well, I can't really recall many dates, times and places about that note in particular. What I do recall are conversations that I had with my investigator on the note, and I further recall several instances where the defense lawyers came to my office in the second story of this building right here, and I opened up my files to them, gave them the whole thing, which included that note along with everything else, photographs, police reports, investigative reports, you name it, I told them they could read what they wanted and they could have copies of about anything they wanted. I wouldn't give them copies of police statements, but I would give them copies of pretty near anything else."

"In the case file was a Xerox copy of that note?"

"Yes, sir. If this is the original sitting in front of me here, it is the first time I've ever seen the original. I don't believe our file contained the original of this note."

"But, as you said, there was a copy in the file?"

"As a matter of fact, I think there was more than one, if I remember correctly."

"And particularly, do you recall Mr. Austin McElroy having an opportunity to peruse the district attorney's file?"

"Yes, sir. On more than one occasion."

"Do you recall ever discussing the note with him prior to the trial?

"I've racked my brains over that. Whether I discussed that note specifically with him, I do recall discussing it on several occasions, more than one time with our investigator, and I do remember doing so with lawyers. Whether I did it specifically with Mr. Austin McElroy, I just simply cannot remember. I really can't. I can't swear that I did. I can't swear that I didn't. I do know the note was in the file and it was handed to him along with the photographs and any other information, evidence, and testimony that we had, he was free to read it and look at it."

When it came turn for Austin McElroy to cross-examine, he asked Herb Alexander no questions.

The State rested with respect to the motion. Austin McElroy called as his witness, Reggie Simmons, the attorney who had represented Joe Vaccaro at trial.

"Before you on the stand is a note that has been marked and placed in evidence. I would ask you if you have ever seen that before?

"I don't believe I have seen the original. I believe that I have either seen a copy of it or I was told what the contents were, but I don't recall whether it was the copy that I saw or that I was told, because, frankly, I just don't recall. I have given my file away to the Public Defender's Office and have not had time to check."

"What would have been the earliest date that you knew of the existence of the note?"

"It would have either been the day the trial began on Monday or the previous Friday. It would have been the day when we had the box of evidence stacked up in the upper courtroom on the jury side of the table and we were going over the evidence, and whichever day that was, the record will reflect, but it was right before the trial on Monday when the trial began."

"Up until that point, you did not know that a note existed?"

"That is correct."

After a brief cross-examination by Bill Alford, the next witness was Thomas Ford.

Tom Ford had been an assistant public defender assigned to help in the defense of Joe Vaccaro.

"Did you know of the existence of that note before trial started?"

"I did not."

"When did you first know about the existence of that note?"

"I can't tell you any kind of date. I can only say that during the course of the trial itself, there was a reference to whether or not Joe Vaccaro could write, and, therefore, if he could write or if he could not write, whether he was capable of writing any kind of communication regarding Faith Hathaway's existence or non-existence. That was the first time that I was aware that something might have occurred, to the best of my recollection now. After that and pursuant to work that you were doing with Robert Lee Willie, I became explicitly aware of the fact there was a note, and it contained these words: 'You never find her.'"

"Who told you about that note?"

"This particular note, to the best of my recollection, you did."

"And would that have been after the trial started?"

"Oh, yeah."

"And particularly, would it have been after the trial was over?"

"Yes."

After Tom Ford finished testifying, the defense rested.

It was now up to Judge Crain whether Willie would get a new trial as a result of the mysterious note. "Based upon the evidence the Court has heard, based upon the evidence the Court heard at the original hearing," Judge Crain said, "the Court does not think that the note adds anything significant one way or the other to the case of the defendant or for that matter to the case of the State. The Court therefore deems it to be insignificant to not in any way create any reasonable doubt as to the guilt of the accused. The Court will deny any motion for a new trial based thereon."

Willie would not get a new trial on his guilt or innocence. His conviction for the first-degree murder of Faith Hathaway would stand. Still, the Louisiana Supreme Court had ordered that Willie receive a new sentencing hearing. It was now time for Willie's second chance to avoid the death penalty to get underway.

WILLIE'S SECOND CHANCE

Willie had a second chance now to avoid the electric chair. He had a brand-new jury, one that not had the chance to sit through a full trial and find him guilty of first-degree murder. In this respect, Willie's odds seemed better than ever that he might yet have the last laugh and avoid the death penalty. The jury in the re-sentencing hearing would decide whether Willie should live or die. And whatever mistakes the defense may have made at trial, they now had the opportunity to learn from them.

The first witness that the State called was Vernon Harvey. It is surreal to hear or read the kind of questions that are asked in criminal trials. Here you have Vernon Harvey, the stepfather of Faith Hathaway, the man who cried a river of tears for his murdered little girl, and approximately two years after Robert Willie and Joe Vaccaro ravaged her body and left her to rot in the woods, Vern Harvey is sitting in a courtroom on a beautiful early summer day, comfortable, and he is asked, "Did you ever know a person by the name of Faith Hathaway?"

His answer is simple and full of irony, "Sure did."

"What relationship was that to you?"

"I raised her from a baby. She was my stepdaughter."

I was the next witness called. I described searching Fricke's Cave and finding Faith's body. I described going to Texarkana and getting Robert Willie's confession. I was asked by Bill Alford, "Do you see Robert Willie in the courtroom today?"

"Yes, sir. I do."

"Would you identify him, please?"

"He is sitting at the end of counsel table with the blue coat on and long blond hair."

"Did you record everything that was said by Robert Willie?"

"No, sir."

"Just tell us how you handled the statement."

"Before I pulled the tape player out, he gave me an oral statement where me and him just talked and where I asked him questions and he would answer."

I played the cassette tape, while each of the jurors was given a transcription of the tape to read.

After a recess, Mr. Paul McGarry, the pathologist who had performed the autopsy on Faith's body, testified. As he had done at the original trial, he testified about the horrible injuries to Faith. The stab wounds, the tearing of her vagina from forcible rape, the bruising and tearing of the skin on the inner parts of her thighs as they were forced apart and as the rape was underway, the defensive wounds to her hand, the cutting of her windpipe that would have eliminated her ability to speak. He said that Faith's death had been both painful and slow as her windpipe filled with blood.

Bill Alford had his secretary, Debbie Mitchell, lie down on the floor, and he positioned her in the position that Faith's body had been found in. "Okay, both her hands up high over her head, palms up, both legs were spread very far apart, just about as far apart as they would go and bent just a little bit up like this."

"Now, Doctor, would you expect that a person that has received the injuries that you observed at autopsy to be found in that position if they had not been held until they were dead or unconscious?"

"No, I would not," Dr. McGarry said. This is in direct conflict with Helen Prejean's supposition in *Dead Man Walking* that Faith moved into the position in which I found her in Fricke's Cave.

"So then would it be your expert opinion that Faith Hathaway was held in that position until she died or became unconscious?" Bill asked.

"Yes, sir."

"The legs being spread that far apart would be an uncomfortable position, would it not?"

"I would expect, yes," Dr. McGarry said.

"Is that one reason that you feel that she was dead when left or unconscious when left in order that they stay that far apart?"

"Yes."

"So then it is your expert opinion that Faith Hathaway was held in that position until she died or until very close to death?" Bill asked.

"Yes."

Bill Alford asked Dr. McGarry where he had found Faith's senior class necklace.

"It was embedded in the neck," Dr. McGarry said. "It was right down in the wound."

On cross-examination, Austin tried to distance the rape from the murder. Since rape was one of the aggravating factors that was required for the murder to produce the death penalty, he was doing what he had to do to try to introduce doubt that the rape was associated in time with the murder.

"Doctor, during your autopsy, was it possible for you to determine when the forcible intercourse took place?" Austin asked.

"I determined that that occurred at or near the time of death because of the nature of the injury to the vagina and the associated areas, showing no signs of healing or anything like that."

"Well, could it have happened say within six hours of what you determined to be the time of death?" Austin asked.

"I would not expect it, because there was no swelling, there was no evidence that it reacted to the injury."

"All right. Is it possible that the injury took place after death?" Austin asked.

"I don't believe so. No, sir. I would expect that this injury would not occur after death, because part of the reason that this injury occurs is the resistance, the attempt to resist the penetration, which causes the tissues to tighten and to resist and to be therefore lacerated. After death there is a tendency for the muscles all to relax, for the tissue to stretch more easily, and I would not expect this to occur at post mortem."

After Dr. McGarry testified, the State rested. Things had gone much faster than anticipated. The State had not brought much of the original evidence to the attention of the jury, although after Dr. McGarry testified, it was all offered into the record for purposes of the record, but the jury neither heard it nor saw it. There had been only three prosecution witnesses: Vern Harvey, Dr. McGarry and me. Four, if you count the actual words of Robert Lee Willie as I played his taped confession to the jury.

Judge Crain adjourned court until 9:30 the next morning. When court reconvened, the defense began its case and its efforts to save Robert Lee Willie from the electric chair.

The first witness that Austin called was Mrs. Hazel Taylor, Robert Lee Willie's aunt.

"Well, my nephew Robert, I've been tending to him off and on ever since he was five years old, and he was off and on from here to there," she said. "I would have him for a while, his mother would have him a while, his grandmother would have him a while, you know, we would each share trying to take care of him and then as he grows older, you know, he began to use drugs, and I talked to him several times about that. I know he was hitting drugs mighty bad."

Hazel Taylor explained that Willie began using drugs when he was about fifteen. She said that Robert's father was in prison and had been there for about twenty years. She blamed Willie's participation in the murder of Faith Hathaway on drugs.

On cross-examination, Bill Alford made the point that neither Hazel Taylor nor anyone in their family ever made Robert Willie take drugs. Rather, it had been his choice to take drugs.

After Hazel Taylor testified, Austin called Robert Lee Willie to take the stand in his own defense. Now, for the first time, Robert Lee Willie would have the chance to make the case for his own life. At the same time, he would make himself available for the first time to the prosecution on cross-examination.

"Robert, you heard the tape recording of your conversation with Michael Varnado and Donald Sharp?" Austin asked.

"Yes, sir."

"I would like you to tell us now in your own words what happened the day before this incident and the day of the incident," Austin said.

"I can't really remember," Willie said.

"Were you doing drugs at this time?"

"Right." Willie said that he was dropping acid, taking Valiums, drinking beer and Jack Daniels.

"I remember when the girl was on the ground, Joe had her head laying in his lap," Willie said. "He had her laid back in his lap. I was standing there, and he pulled out the knife and cut the girl's throat and she moved. She went to get up or something, you know. I grabbed her hand and I let her go. Something just clicked. I seen all the blood and everything, you know."

"So when Joe cut her throat, she was sitting down, is that correct?" Austin asked.

"Yes, sir."

"And it was at that point that she tried to get up and you grabbed her wrists, her hands?"

"Yes, sir," Willie said. "I just grabbed her for an instant and I guess Joe, you know, pulled her back down. I let her go and I just stood there, you know."

"Do you know why the girl was blindfolded?" Austin asked.

"I thought that he blindfolded her so she wouldn't know where she was going, wouldn't be able to find her way out," Willie said.

Austin asked Willie if he had told Faith to "behave" as her throat was being cut.

"I don't remember. I might have been talking to Joe," Willie said.

"Up until the time Joe Vaccaro actually cut her throat, did you know that he planned to kill her?" Austin asked.

"No," Willie said.

"Joe had sexual intercourse with the girl up on top of the hill, is that correct?" Austin asked.

"Yes."

"And you walked down the hill with Joe and the girl?"

"Yes, sir.

"You actually held her hand so that she wouldn't fall, is that correct?" Austin asked.

"Yes, sir."

"Robert, in this statement you made, there is absolutely no indication you tried to stop Joe from doing what he did," Austin said.

"Well, it's a lot different when somebody has got a gun and a knife, you know," Willie said.

"Joe had a gun?" Austin asked.

"Yes, sir."

"Does it bother you what happened?" Austin asked.

"Yes, sir. I'm really sorry that it happened, and I think about it a lot and it worries me, you know, and knowing that I'll never get out of prison, you know, it even bothers me more," Willie said.

On cross-examination, Bill Alford picked up on the last statement made by Robert Willie. "You say it worries you, Robert, that you will probably never get out of prison?"

"Yes, sir."

"Does it worry you that Faith Hathaway will never see the sun rise again?" Bill asked.

"Yes, sir. I am sorry it happened."

"And you think that's enough, I guess, it's enough to be sorry?" Bill asked.

"Do you realize that the testimony of Dr. McGarry makes you a bald-faced liar?" Bill asked. "You say Joe Vaccaro had her head in his lap?"

"Yes, sir."

"Well, don't you realize from Dr. McGarry's testimony you had to be the one between her legs holding her legs open?" Bill asked.

"No. When I grabbed her hands, my legs were straddling her

legs. Because when she went to get up she closed both her legs and done like that to try to get up."

"Didn't you hear Dr. McGarry testify that her legs were as wide apart as they could be?" Bill asked.

"I heard him, yeah."

"Did you hear him say that she had to be held until she was dead or near death in order for her body to be found in the condition that it was found in?" Bill asked.

"When we left her, I think she was still alive," Willie said.

"So you dispute the testimony of the doctor?" Bill asked.

"He wasn't there. I was."

"But the body was there, too," Bill said.

"Yes, sir."

Bill next moved to a description of the crimes Willie and Vaccaro committed against Debbie Cuevas and Mark Brewster. He noted that these crimes occurred only three days after the murder of Faith Hathaway.

"You would have this jury believe that you were shocked and you freaked out over what Joe Vaccaro did to faith Hathaway?" Bill asked.

"Yes, sir."

"And yet you're right back with him two or three days and you are doing similar things?" Bill asked.

"Well, I looked at it this way. I knowed about it and he knowed about it. I couldn't turn my back on him. If I had went to the police, I would have probably got killed," Willie said.

"So you just decided to continue raping and kidnapping with Joe Vaccaro?" Bill asked.

"Yes, sir," Willie said.

As Bill closed his cross-examination of Willie, he said, "You say that you believe that when you left Faith Hathaway she was alive?"

"Yes, sir."

"Did it occur to you that you weren't very far from a hospital? Did it occur to you that maybe you ought to try to take the girl to the hospital, help the girl?" Bill asked.

"All I wanted to do was get out of there," Willie said.

"And you didn't care about her?" Bill asked.

"I cared about myself," Willie said.

"That is still about all you care about, too, isn't it?"

"That's right," Willie said, his face set in a glare at Bill Alford. Finally, the truth from Robert Lee Willie.

Bill glared back at Willie. "I don't have any other questions."

Austin McElroy asked no questions on re-direct. The defense rested.

After a brief recess, Bill Alford began his closing argument. As Bill had done when he argued the case against Joe Vaccaro, he used the metaphor of Faith's body speaking—screaming—to the jury, telling them what had happened to her.

"There is an old saying that dead men tell no tales, but you've seen in this case that that's not true," Bill said. "Faith Hathaway's body screams out a message to you. She's dead. Her body screams to you, and it screams because we can show you the way she was found."

He paused, slowly pacing in front of the jury box, looking at each of the jurors. "First of all, her body is telling you that she struggled, that she fought, that she did her best she could to try to save her own life. The marks between her legs and the tear in her vagina are all the evidence and proof positive that she struggled for her life. That she struggled to keep from being raped. The injury to her vagina was the result of her struggling, of her fighting, her fighting to keep her from being raped, and her fighting for her life, and it's unmistakable and her body told you that."

Bill continued. "Her body tells you something else, too. It tells you, ladies and gentlemen, it took two people to kill her. That's the reason I'm like this, and two people held me until I died or until I was near death, too near to move. Allow yourself to imagine the sounds that were probably coming from Faith Hathaway when she was struggling for her breath and her heart is becoming her own worst enemy and is pumping her life's blood out of her body. It would be very, very painful. It's not an instant death. It's not a very sudden unconsciousness, like a blow to the head."

In his brief closing argument, Austin asked the jury not to seek vengeance. He argued that Willie demonstrated that he did not intend for Faith to die because he had helped her down the hill at Fricke's Cave.

After Austin completed his argument, Bill Alford stood up and faced the jury for the last time in this case. He would have the last word. "We do have a tendency to forget the dead," he said. "We have a tendency to forget that Faith Hathaway had a right to live. Faith Hathaway had a right to walk the streets of Mandeville. She wasn't doing anything illegal. She has a right, had a right to be here today. She never got an opportunity to have lawyers and jurors sit in judgment on her. Robert Willie and Joe Vaccaro were her judges and jury and executioner."

Bill paused for emphasis. "Do you think she was scared? Do you think she was frightened? Do you think she wanted to cry? Do you think maybe she wanted to say, 'Momma, help me. Somebody help me.' Do you think she suffered? What did Robert Willie do to help her then?"

Bill closed his argument by asserting that the death penalty would affirm the value of Faith's life. "When the evidence is as strong as it is in this case, the only punishment is death. And why? Why is that? Why is the only punishment death? Because if we as a community, if you as a group of citizens are going to say that life is valuable, you are going to say that Faith Hathaway had a right to live. If you're going to hold anything holy about the life of Faith Hathaway, if you're going to say that it has any value at all, you've got to say the death penalty, because otherwise you're saying, Robert Willie, your life is more valuable than Faith Hathaway's, your life means more than Faith Hathaway."

Bill thanked the jury and sat down. Judge Crain instructed the jury on the law and the jury retired to deliberate at 11:21 in the morning. At 12:49, the jury returned with a verdict, having been out for only one hour and twenty-eight minutes. Again, the verdict was death.

"Let the record show in the matter of State of Louisiana versus Robert Lee Willie," Judge Crain said, "the defendant having been convicted by a jury of having committed the crime of first-degree murder, the defendant having been sentenced to death by a subsequent sentencing jury, the defendant being present in open court in person and through counsel—what are you, twenty-three, Mr. Willie?"

"Twenty-four."

"The defendant having stated to the court he is twenty-four years of age, the Court orders that the defendant be remanded to the Department of Corrections to be placed in their custody until the Supreme Court reviews the capital sentence herein, that upon being affirmed, a warrant issue from this court ordering the Department of Corrections to place the defendant in the electric chair and to put him to death as provided by law."

HEMBY AND WAGNER: WILLIE COPS A PLEA

When the Louisiana Supreme Court granted Robert Willie a second chance to avoid the electric chair for the murder of Faith Hathaway, fully four years had come and gone since Dennis Hemby had disappeared from the Tavern Lounge in Covington.

During a lunch break on June 29, 1982, the second day of Willie's re-sentencing hearing, he told Sergeant Donald Sharp that there was something he wanted to discuss with him. Donald Sharp remembered that Joe Vaccaro had wanted to talk to him just days after Vaccaro and Willie had killed Faith Hathaway. Perhaps Willie, like Vaccaro, had something he wanted to get off his chest. Sergeant Sharp could not have been prepared for the surprise in store for him when Willie told him that he and his cousin, Perry, had participated in the drowning and robbing of Dennis Hemby.

Willie told Sharp that his cousin had pulled a knife on Hemby and had pushed him down into the river and drowned him while Willie merely stood by. Willie also said that it was his cousin who had taken Hemby's money off of his dead body and then split the money—approximately $300—with Willie. Willie said that he and his cousin also divided up Hemby's stash of marijuana.

Based on the information supplied by Willie, the authorities were able to locate the skeletal remains of Dennis Hemby near the river outside Covington where they had lain undiscovered for over four years. As a result of the subsequent investigation, Perry Taylor was questioned. He told the authorities that it was

Willie who had attacked Hemby and drowned him, as described earlier in this book.

On September 13, 1982, Robert Lee Willie pled guilty to the reduced charge of second-degree murder in the death of Dennis Hemby and was sentenced to life in prison. This was in addition to Willie's three life sentences in the federal system, four life sentences in Louisiana for kidnapping and rape, and his death sentence.

During the time that Willie was in jail in St. Tammany Parish immediately before his re-sentencing hearing and after it, he developed an unusual relationship with Lat McNeese, Chief Investigator for the Washington Parish Sheriff's Office. Lat had been the one who had traveled to the federal prison in Marion, Illinois, to bring Willie back to Louisiana for his re-sentencing hearing.

Lat spent quite a bit of time with Willie, both at the jail and in transporting him from jail to the Washington Parish courthouse in connection with the re-sentencing hearing. They talked a lot. Once Lat asked Willie about a chain with five skulls on it that was tattooed on Willie's left wrist. Willie told Lat that each of the skulls represented a person whom Willie had killed.

Perhaps it was this statement that led Willie to tell Lat about his other victims. Over a period of time, Willie told Lat about his involvement in the June 3, 1978, murder of St. Tammany Parish Deputy Louis Wagner II. This information led to the arrest of the other three men involved in addition to Willie.

Bill Alford interviewed Willie in great detail after he told McNeese of his involvement in the killing of Sergeant Wagner. Willie even gave a sworn statement in August 1982, not long before he pled guilty to the killing of Dennis Hemby, implicating himself and his three accomplices in Wagner's murder. The killing took place substantially as described earlier in this book.

Robert Willie even testified before the Grand Jury with respect to Sergeant Wagner's murder, but he later recanted his confession after the infamous serial killer, Henry Lee Lucas, who murdered approximately three hundred sixty people as he crisscrossed the country, claimed to have killed Sergeant Wagner.

Willie told investigators that he had confessed merely to be able to stay for a longer time in the St. Tammany Parish jail after his re-sentencing hearing where he thought he might be able to escape—he had once escaped from there earlier. It has been reported also that Willie recanted only after his father, John Willie, told him that he was violating the code of honor among criminals by implicating the other three men.

It was later determined that Lucas and Otis Toole, a Florida convict and occasional travelling companion of Lucas, who also had confessed to Wagner's murder, could not have been involved. Willie pled guilty to the second-degree murder of Louis Wagner on August 4, 1983, and was sentenced to an additional life in prison. All in all, Willie now had been sentenced to nine consecutive life sentences and one sentence of death.

In speaking of the times he spent talking with Willie, McNeese told a local newspaper that, "He also told me that he killed a guy that was driving a brick truck in St. Tammany Parish. He robbed him, and he wasn't going to kill him, but the guy threw a brick through his windshield so he ran over him and killed him." McNeese said Willie told him that he disposed of the body in a pond along the interstate.

McNeese said Willie also told him that he had once killed a hitchhiker, but he never revealed any more details about that particular murder.

An unknown hitchhiker, the driver of a brick truck, Louis Wagner, Dennis Hemby, and Faith Hathaway—five deaths, five skulls on Willie's prison tattoo.

FINAL APPEALS

After Willie was sentenced to death for the second time in July 1982 for the murder of Faith Hathaway, he began the process of appealing his conviction and his sentence. Usually this process takes a number of years. It is not unusual for death sentences to languish in the courts for more than a decade. The length of time between a sentence of death and the carrying out of that sentence is not really surprising. A defendant sentenced to death has several layers of appeals. First, the state courts review the conviction and death sentence. Then, review is sought in the United States Supreme Court. Habeas corpus petitions follow, first in the state courts and then in the federal courts.

In Robert Willie's case, however, the time between his sentence of death in July 1982 and his execution on December 28, 1984, was approximately thirty months. According to Bill Alford, the prosecutor who obtained the death sentence against Willie that was ultimately carried out, this represents the second shortest time between sentence and execution in Louisiana history. Alford credits the relative lightning-speed pace of Willie's appeals to the diligent efforts and skilled 'lawyering' of J. Kevin McNary, then a young prosecutor in District Attorney Marion Farmer's office. According to Bill Alford, McNary's brief-writing style was exemplary, and he showed himself to be Robert Lee Willie's worst nightmare.

After Willie finally exhausted all of his judicial avenues in late 1984, it became clear that he would finally pay for his crimes with his life. Robert Lee Willie, who once boasted that he would never be executed for murdering Faith Hathaway, must have been amazed by the intensity of the fight brought to bear against him.

THE PARDON HEARING

After both the state and federal courts, including the United States Supreme Court, had denied all of Willie's claims, there was little left to Willie but to seek mercy from the five members of the Louisiana Board of Pardons. The pardon hearing was held on November 19, 1984, in an auditorium inside the Louisiana State Penitentiary at Angola, where Willie had been on death row for more than a year—ever since he had been transported from the St. Tammany Parish jail after his guilty plea in August 1983 for the murder of Sergeant Louis Wagner.

Willie's request to the Board of Pardons was simple—spare his life and permit him to serve out his life in prison. Whatever the Board of Pardons decided, it would represent merely a recommendation to Louisiana Governor Edwin Edwards. Ultimately, it was up to the Governor whether Willie would live or die. However, since Governor Edwards would never override the Board of Pardons if it voted in opposition to Willie's request for clemency, the Board of Pardons represented Willie's last viable chance to avoid death in the electric chair.

I attended the pardon hearing with Bill Alford, who had prosecuted Joe Vaccaro and had succeeded in obtaining the death penalty for Willie in Willie's re-sentencing trial. Marion Farmer, the district attorney who had prosecuted Willie, handled the State's case against Willie and did a great job laying out the strong grounds for upholding the sentence of the jury and proceeding with the execution. He told the Board that Willie had "given up his right to live on this earth." He also invited the Board to give Willie "the same consideration he gave Faith Hathaway."

When it came time for Willie to speak, he made a long, rambling speech, although, even then, he refused to beg for his life. He said, "My death is not going to bring Miss Hathaway back to this earth." As he had during his trial, Willie said that his only part in the murder was holding Faith down while Joe Vaccaro actually killed her.

I sat quietly during the proceeding not far from Mr. and Mrs. Harvey. I remember looking at Helen Prejean who was sitting by Willie holding his hand at times. She was wearing a dark blue suit and a ruffled blouse. She touched Willie on the shoulder when he was brought into the room in shackles, and during the hearing she brought him a cup of coffee.

After Willie testified, his mother came up to the table where Willie sat and sat down beside him. She did not look at him as she spoke. She said simply, "He was always a good boy." Then she began to cry and got up and went back to a seat in the back of the room.

After both Willie and his mother had spoken, Helen Prejean spoke on Willie's behalf. Her presentation was by far the longest one of the day. She argued that Willie was not fully responsible for his actions because he was drunk and on drugs at the time of the murder.

The hearing took two hours, about twenty minutes of which represented the time that the board deliberated before reaching its decision. Indeed, the Board of Pardons was not even out long enough for Bill and me to smoke a cigarette in the hallway. Their decision was hardly surprising. The Board was unanimous in refusing to recommend to the Governor that he grant a pardon to Willie. Willie's time to meet death had come. His execution would proceed.

On November 21, Judge France Watts set the execution date for Willie as December 28, echoing the date of Faith Hathaway's murder, May 28. The date of Willie's execution, December 28, 1984, was actually the fourth scheduled date set for his execution. On two previous occasions, the execution had been stayed as a result of legal maneuvering on the part of Willie's defense team. The third time, the scheduled execution date was postponed by the action of Governor Edwin Edwards, who had given Willie a fifteen-day reprieve less than twenty-four hours before the date scheduled for him to die in order to allow him to present his case before the Board of Pardons. Now that the Board had spoken, Willie's time had finally come.

DEATH ROW ON THE FARM

The Louisiana State Penitentiary at Angola, the only maximum-security prison in the State and one of the largest prisons in the country, is located about an hour's drive northwest of Baton Rouge. A metal roof covers a small guardhouse at the entrance to the prison, forming what looks like a large carport over the road. Stop signs on the end of long poles keep cars from entering or leaving the prison grounds without the approval of the guards keeping watch and who manually raise and lower the poles to allow cars through the gate. The guards themselves, dressed in black uniforms with large red patches in the shape of Louisiana on their shoulders, are friendly and efficient. They seem quite used to letting a steady stream of traffic in and out of the prison.

The prison buildings are predominantly yellow, trimmed in reddish-brown. The first building inside to the main gate, just to the right of the highway, is the Reception Center. It is here that new prisoners arrive to be processed and then classified. The Reception Center is also home to Death Row. To enter the Reception Center, you have to pass through two separate chain-link fences that are approximately twelve to fifteen feet in height. The first fence is strung, top and bottom, with razor wire. The second fence is topped with razor wire.

Once inside the second chain-link fence, you find yourself in a beautifully landscaped yard. There is a concrete walkway bordered by flowers, and near the door of the building is a small pond with a fountain on which a host of brown ducks swim and quack happily, unaware that they are residents of Death Row.

Once inside the building, you have the office of the assistant warden, Warden Lee, who is in charge of Death Row. Each camp within the prison has its own assistant warden in charge of that group of men. Warden Lee, a small, but muscular and no-nonsense African-American man in his early fifties, runs the row efficiently and with a military bearing. He is friendly and kind to the staff and to the prisoners. "I'm a soldier," he says. Although chain-link fencing and razor wire surround each camp within Angola with guard towers in the corners of the perimeter of each fence, Warden Lee says, "It is not walls that keep men in. It's people."

In order to pass into the actual living area of Death Row, one must pass first through a sliding barred door, where the gaps between the bars are covered with a thick network of wire. Once past this door, you find yourself in a hall approximately ninety feet long. The floor is terrazzo and polished to a mirror sheen. The walls are greenish tile. The place has the appearance and even the cleanliness of a hospital. It is also very quiet and peaceful—no loud noises, no yelling, no clanging of gates. Almost like a library or a church.

To the right at the end of this hall is another sliding barred gate with the same wire mesh. A metal detector is set up a few feet in front of this door. If the barred door is opened to you and you walk through, you find yourself on Death Row.

Death Row is made of seven tiers—A through G. Each tier has fifteen cells, except for one that has only eleven. In addition, there is a cell at the end of each hallway that contains a shower-head and serves as the tier's shower room. In all, there are 101 inmate cells on Death Row.

On a recent visit I made to Death Row, there were eighty-seven inmates residing on the Row. One arrived while I was there, having been sentenced for murdering his mother-in-law at home, then going to a church service and killing his wife, his two-year-old son, and another individual. This prisoner was shot by police and paralyzed from the neck down. His cell was modified to allow for his handicapped status while he awaited death by lethal injection. I said, "He has already been punished for his crime." Warden Lee looked directly at me and said, "Not enough yet."

The hall on which I stood was curved, with a tier on each side. There would be tiers above and tiers on the other wing of Death Row, all the same thoughout. I went through another barred door, this time without mesh and was immediately in the presence of the Death Row inmates. A row of fifteen cells stretched before me to my right, beginning after the shower room, which also was fronted by bars.

The first cell is cell number 1. This is the cell that a man is moved to when he is on deathwatch prior to being moved to the cell in the death house near the death chamber. In this way, he is only a few feet from the gate where the guards are, and so he can be more easily observed and monitored.

The cells themselves are six feet by nine feet, so the length of the hallway of the tier is about ninety feet long, the distance between home plate and first base. You can walk past each of these fifteen cells in a minute until you reach the end and turn around. The cells are clean and, as might be expected, quite Spartan. There is a bunk attached to the wall, a metal shelf on which a thin mattress pad of green material is spread. Next to the bed in the rear of the cell are a toilet and a sink. There is a small table near the front of the cell.

As I walked down Death Row, I noticed that most of the inmates were in their white boxer shorts. It was hot, and they were either lying on their cots or on the floor beside their cots, sleeping or resting or doing what men do who are locked up all day long, every day. A few of the inmates will stare at visitors, but most do not. A visitor to Death Row is almost always struck by the similarly to the lion house at the zoo as he strolls down the row, looking in. Predators, each and every one, kept from us by bars, but reduced to sluggish and hypnotically boring existences by being caged away.

On my recent visit, one man is dressed in full-prison garb, a white shirt and white pants. His eyes are wide and crazed. He stands at the bars, sticking his arms through as I pass, whispering, "My cell is on fire. Help me, please." I am careful to stay out of his grasp, which is not that easy because the hallway on the Row is narrow.

The hallway is floored in concrete, painted gray. Like the rest of the prison, it is hospital clean. It is probably no more than six feet wide. On the left, immediately facing the cells are windows. Death Row at Angola is not a window-less dungeon, not what one might imagine. On sunny days, the tier is bright. There is glass on the windows, of course, but the windows swing open on hinges at the bottom so that the sounds of birds can be heard. You can smell the grass and the trees, a gentle breeze brings the inmates the sweet smell of the Louisiana countryside, and if a strong enough breeze blows, maybe even the smell of the Mississippi River nearby.

Outside the window on the tier is a yard in which one small fenced area is set up for each of the cells on the tier. One walks out of the tier into the yard, and then one enters one of these fenced areas that begins with a gate and then gets wider in a triangular shape. It is approximately ninety feet long, narrowed to a point at the gate and only about ten feet wide at the back, its widest point. There is a concrete walk in the middle and a little bit of grass off the walk where a prisoner can touch the grass. Each exercise area looks like a dog run. Each has a basketball goal at the wide end in the rear. There is no roof on the exercise area, but the entire fenced-in area is topped by a row of razor wire. Only a few feet separate each caged area.

Warden Lee says that they don't use a real basketball anymore because it is too expensive. Instead they use a nerf basketball. Only one inmate is allowed in the exercise yard at a time, and he is shackled even when he is out in the yard, both his feet and his hands. However, the chain attached to his wrists is long enough to allow a man to shoot baskets if he chooses. Warden Lee says that some can shoot the ball like Michael Jordan even shackled hand and foot.

Death Row inmates are kept in their cells twenty-three hours each day. The single hour a day they are allowed to leave their cells is to be used to take a shower or simply move up and down the tier in the hall under the guard of a security officer.

Three times a week, the inmates are allowed an hour in the yard. They are also allowed unlimited access to visitors. They meet with their attorneys in the attorney call-out room, which is on the main hallway between the two barred and meshed gates. It is a large room with a wooden table with a high middle that keeps the lawyers on one side and the inmates on the other. A guard stands watch just outside the door, and he can see through the small window in the door. On the wall are two murals painted in 1998 by one of the inmates who has painted murals throughout the common areas of the prison, such as the chapel. The two murals are of a cabin on a lake with birds and trees, a pastoral scene. The other scene is a cartoon of a large Scooby Doo, grinning out at you.

Restrictions include no plastic or glass containers, one personal call a month for five minutes, only a certain number of books at one time, no tape player, no contact visits except that contact visits with attorneys were allowed beginning in January 1991.

You hear people who oppose the death penalty in all its forms and shapes say that life in prison without probation or parole is sufficient to protect the general population. Putting aside the possibility that an inmate might receive a pardon from a governor and without taking into account the danger that some men pose to the other inmates, you have to realize that escape is a possibility, even on Death Row. It has happened at Angola.

A little before midnight on November 3, 1999, four murderers awaiting execution on Angola's Death Row sawed through the bars of one of the windows facing the tier with hacksaw blades that had been smuggled into Death Row. The men escaped into the yard beyond. They were free of Death Row for about three hours, although they never made it off the prison property. In one respect, it is probably a safeguard that the main gate with all its guards is adjacent to Death Row. On the other hand, if an inmate can make it out of the building and can get past the two chain-link fences, he would essentially be loose on the highway.

After the escapees were recaptured and returned to Death Row, guards discovered ropes made from bed sheets, knapsacks made from blue jeans, and a raft made from plastic milk cartons that the men apparently intended to use to cross the Mississippi River that flows by the prison. The men also had paramilitary training books, a map and a thousand dollars in cash.

The death chamber is housed in Camp F. All the inmates in Camp F are trustees, the most trusted and least dangerous of the inmates. These inmates take food to the other inmates, mop floors, and perform other support tasks around the prison. Near Camp F is a small lake where trustees can fish. I myself have fished here under the leaves of abundant pecan trees. Scarcely a hundred feet away is the place of death.

Just prior to an execution, the warden will have the condemned man transferred from his cell on Death Row to a cell near the death chamber in Camp F. Only the warden knows exactly when the man is to be brought over for security reasons and in order not to upset the general feelings on Death Row. It is usually early the day of the execution or the day before. Executions can be carried out at any time on the scheduled execution day between 6:00 p.m. and midnight. Often the rest of the prison is unaware that an execution is occurring. According to Warden Lee, though, the Death Row inmates have a change in mood after they lose one of their own. "The men get a little quieter after an execution. It suddenly becomes more real to them."

In speaking to Warden Lee about Robert Lee Willie, he said, "I was supervisor of classification in 1984 when Robert was executed. I remember meeting with him about a week or so before the execution to discuss his wishes for his remains."

I was curious if Willie had shown any remorse as he approached death, if he said anything that would lead you to believe he was sorry for the pain he had caused. The warden shook his head. "No. About all he said was that people said he had killed that girl, and now they were going to kill him. He said that killing was wrong, no matter who did it."

Robert Lee Willie arrived on Death Row at Angola on November 7, 1983. Even after two trials that both resulted in a sentence of death, I think he was still surprised to find himself on Death Row. As a result of his federal convictions for kidnapping and the three life sentences he was sentenced to serve in federal prison, he did not think that he would be brought to Louisiana to face his own personal judgment day. He thought he would live out his days in the federal prison in Marion, Illinois. Willie did not take into account the tenacity of our district attorney, Marion Farmer, and of the entire prosecution team.

Marion contacted our local congressman, Bob Livingston, who briefly was slated to become Speaker of the House during the presidency of Bill Clinton before Congressman Livingston stepped aside in favor of Dennis Hastert. The federal government was pleased to cooperate with us. In fact, Vernon Harvey received a personal call from President Reagan, who told Mr. Harvey that Willie was going to be returned to Louisiana to face execution.

I had to fly to Marion, Illinois, with a court order and finger-print cards, and ID's of the police officers who were going to be transporting Willie back to Louisiana. Once I flew to Marion and gave the fingerprint cards, court order, and ID's, I came back home. Lat McNeese, who was Chief Investigator for the Washington Parish Sheriff's Office, and my father, Harold Varnado, Sr., who worked for the Franklinton Police Department, then drove to Marion, Illinois, and transported Willie from the federal prison there back to Franklinton in the summer of 1982 prior to his re-sentencing hearing. The prison personnel in Marion actually got a fingerprint expert to com-pare the cards I had taken earlier to the actual fingerprints of Lat and my father. I sent the two people I trusted most in the world to do the job. I did not want Willie to escape.

Once Willie arrived at Angola, he spent the next three hun-dred ten days on Death Row. Approximately six weeks before his execution, he met Helen Prejean there. On Christmas Eve in 1984, he was moved to Camp F and the deathwatch began.

WITNESS TO AN EXECUTION

Louisiana State Penitentiary at Angola. Friday, December 27, 1984.
Robert Willie looks at the large pile of food that has been set in
front of him—fried fish, oysters, shrimp, French fries and salad.
"Too bad you have to die to get food like this," he thinks. He picks
up a shrimp and pops it into his mouth. He closes his eyes and
concentrates on the flavor of one of his favorite foods, holding the
shrimp for a long time before chewing and swallowing. He takes
his time as he eats, wishing he could will the hands on the clock
to stop in their relentless sweep. It won't be long now.

Just a few weeks ago, Willie had given an interview to the State-
Times, a newspaper in Baton Rouge, in which he said, "When my
time comes, my problems will be over with. I won't have to be
told when to eat, when to sleep. I won't have to worry when my
time comes on the twenty-eighth."

He also told the interviewer, "I can't go back and change
nothing. I'm an outlaw. I've been an outlaw most of my life. If I
had it to do all over again, I'd be an outlaw. I've lived a pretty
good life. I've done almost everything there is to do—drugs, sex,
rock 'n roll, travel, football, school—about everything. So I'm
ready. I'm ready."

John Willie, Robert's father, also has been speaking to the
press in recent days. The elder Willie served time in Angola for
aggravated battery, manslaughter and cattle theft, but he was
released in October 1983, just a month before Robert Willie
came to Angola's Death Row. He reportedly told a reporter that

he believed that Willie and Vaccaro both deserved to die for their crimes. He said that he strongly supported the death penalty, even going so far to say that he would be willing to pull the switch himself. At one point, John Willie even claimed to have wired the electric chair at Angola in which his son was scheduled to be executed, saying that he had done the work while he was an inmate electrician. He would later admit that he had not taken part in wiring the electric chair.

While the minutes tick down for Robert Lee Willie, Bill Alford and I make our way to Angola. As we round a curve in the road, I can see the front gate of the Louisiana State Penitentiary in the distance. It has been only five weeks since I was last here at Robert Lee Willie's pardon hearing. Now, I am here with Bill Alford to witness his execution in the electric chair. The ride from Franklinton to Angola has been uneventful. Bill and I have chatted about everything and nothing. Mostly, we have avoided speaking about what we have driven about 140 miles to see—the death of Robert Lee Willie.

As we pull up to the guardhouse at the front gate, I can see that it is draped in red Christmas ribbons. I am reminded that only a handful of days remain in the year. My attendance at Willie's execution will be my last assignment for the District Attorney's Office. On January 1, Walter Reed will succeed Marion Farmer as Washington Parish District Attorney.

The guard checks his clipboard and finds our names on the list of the official witnesses to Willie's execution. He waves us in. The sun is just beginning to set as we slowly drive the short distance to the squat, nondescript building where the execution will be carried out.

The warden greets us as we enter the building. A table has been laid out with sandwiches and snacks. Bill helps himself, but I decide against it. I really don't feel like eating. Instead, I decide to take a walk outside.

There is a lake near the death house, and it is here that I stroll in the approaching dusk. I am alone with my thoughts. Mostly, I think of the changes my life has undergone in the past four years since that afternoon in early June 1980 when I received the telephone call from Richard Newman telling me of the discovery of Faith Hathaway's clothing and personal items in Fricke's Cave. I was so full of piss and vinegar back then, so full of dreams and trust. Now, I am tired and burned out, glad to be out of the District Attorney's Office for good.

As I stand on the bank of the twenty-acre lake, I watch in silence as the sun falls for the final time in the life of Robert Lee Willie. The sky turns from golden to red and then to a ruddy gray. As the light fades from the day, the jade-colored water from the lake reflects the huge cypress trees, giving them the appearance of being painted on the lake's surface. Beautiful cypress stumps line the banks of the lake, protruding up through its painted surface, adding a three-dimensional effect to the picture.

For a brief moment, my mind travels back to the last time I stood beside this lake. Lat McNeese and I had come fishing a few months after the murder trials, and it was only on my way out, after spending a very relaxed and peaceful day with my friend catching a stringer full of white perch, that he pointed and reminded me that the death house was close by. This time things are much different.

A couple of minutes before midnight we are escorted to the witness room that is adjacent to the death chamber. The witness room is small, only about eight by twelve feet. As we enter, I see that someone has lined up six red plastic chairs in a single row. Elizabeth and Vern Harvey sit in the chairs farthest from the door. Two reporters take the seats next to the Harveys. Bill Alford takes the next seat, and I sit in the seat at the end of the row closest to the door.

Robert Lee Willie runs his hand over his head. It is smooth to the touch. Just a few minutes before, he had been taken from his holding cell to a place where a man had shaved his head. Even his eyebrows had been shaved. The lower part of the left leg of his pants had been cut off and the barber had shaved the lower part of his left leg. Before being taken back to his cell, he had been fitted with a diaper. Willie thinks back to the interview he gave to the reporter from the Times Picayune in New Orleans. He had told the man that if he were free he would be a terrorist, relishing the destruction of government buildings. Now, here he is, shaved for slaughter and wearing a diaper like a baby.

In a small booth adjacent to the death chamber stands the executioner, although his official title is the more benign "electrician." His real identity is secret. When he is referred to by name, he is called Sam Jones, an alias that is derived from the name of the Governor of Louisiana at the time that the electric chair was first put to use in the state. Sam Jones will receive his usual paycheck of $400 for pushing the button that will begin the process of electrocuting Robert Lee Willie. If you saw him on the street, he would not stand out from the crowd. He has blue eyes, and his red hair is beginning to turn gray. Tonight, after Willie is dead, Sam Jones will return to his home where he will take an artist's brush in hand, just as he does after each execution. He will not be ready for sleep. Instead, he will allow his mind to wander far from the death chamber at Angola as, in the stillness of night, he paints and tries to create something of beauty.

It is now almost midnight. I am sitting in the small plastic chair near the door in the witness room. Bill Alford, the reporters and the Harveys are sitting as well, waiting. In front of us, only six feet away on the other side of a large glass window, sits the electric chair. It is made of solid oak and is quite large. On the wall behind the chair is a giant exhaust fan that is spinning frantically. Beside the fan on the wall is a red telephone. I do not expect the phone to ring tonight.

The assistant warden enters the room and begins to explain

precisely how the execution will be carried out. "As you can see," he says, "there are six straps on the chair. On the strap-down team, there is a guard assigned to each of the straps."

As he speaks, I can see the electrician in the booth behind him fiddling with a series of large dials and switches. He continues, "You will see what appears to be smoke coming from different parts of the prisoner's body, but I assure you that this is just the saline solution evaporating from the skin of the condemned."

After the basic details have been laid out, Warden Frank Blackburn steps forward and looks solemnly at each of us. "You are here as witnesses only," he says. "You are not to speak or make any comment whatsoever during the execution. Please maintain your silence at all times while you are in this room. We won't tolerate any disturbance in here. Anybody who violates this rule will be escorted out."

A few moments later, as the rest of the witnesses sit quietly, I hear a sound over my shoulder. It is Helen Prejean. She has come into the room and is standing right behind me. She must not have been paying attention to Warden Blackburn's admonition to remain silent, as she has begun to pray out loud. Her voice is not a mere whisper. She is speaking quietly, but clearly and distinctly, and I know that everyone in the room can hear her. Her words are in the form of a prayer, but it is an indictment, an accusation that she is uttering. "Please forgive these people," she is saying. "Please forgive them for collaborating in the killing of this man."

Instantly, I am outraged. Only a few feet away sit Elizabeth and Vern Harvey. Do they have to be accused of complicity in Robert Lee Willie's death as they await the final moment of justice for their daughter's killer? I want to stand up and tell Helen Prejean to be quiet. In the end, I take a deep breath and hold my tongue.

At 12:01 A.M., Warden Blackburn gives a signal for Willie to be brought to the death chamber. A few moments later, Willie enters the room after walking approximately fifty feet from his cell to the death chamber. The six members of the strap-down team surround him. On his legs are shackles. On his wrists are handcuffs. He is dressed in blue jeans and a tight, white tee shirt. The left leg of his blue jeans has been cut off at the knee to allow for the electrode to be affixed to his leg. On his feet, he wears white hospital slippers.

Willie's body is covered with almost thirty tattoos, including a peacock, marijuana leaves, and a bracelet of skulls. A separate letter is tattooed on the fingers of one of his hands, near the knuckles, spelling out the word "love." Beneath the tee shirt, after he was sentenced to death, Willie had the grim reaper holding a knife and an hourglass tattooed on his chest.

Upon entering the room, the strap down team walks Willie up to a small podium near the glass window. He is only a few feet away from us as he stands at the podium. He speaks into a small microphone that has been fitted on the podium. His voice is filled with anger, with no trace of remorse. He looks directly ahead, avoiding eye contact with any of us, including Elizabeth and Vern Harvey.

"I would just like to say, Mr. and Mrs. Harvey, that I hope you get some relief from my death." He is speaking slowly and deliberately. His face is tight, and I can feel the hatred bubbling just below the surface of his words.

"Killing people is wrong," he says. "That's why you've put me to death. It makes no difference whether it's citizens, countries or governments, killing is wrong."

Having said his final words, Willie turns and immediately walks to the electric chair surrounded by the six guards of the strap-down team. His feet barely touch the ground, in reality, as he is guided to the chair by the guards.

Willie is placed in the chair, and the guards quickly strap him in. An electrode is attached to his exposed left leg. Another is attached to the top of his head.

It is now time for the leather hood to be placed over Willie's face. At this moment, I see a small tear roll down Willie's right cheek. He winks at Helen Prejean. Immediately, the dampened hood is dropped in place. It occurs to me that the last view of the world that Faith had before she died was the canopy of trees overhead her as she lay struggling for breath on the sandy floor of Fricke's Cave. Robert Lee Willie's last view of the world was the dark inside of a leather mask.

One of the guards pulls the chinstrap tight. Willie's head jerks back against the back of the chair.

"Everybody ready?" Warden Blackburn asks. Now that the moment of Willie's death has arrived, I can feel my heart beating so hard in my chest that I am afraid I might be having a heart attack.

The Warden signals Sam Jones, the electrician. He pushes a button, and immediately two thousand volts of electricity course through Robert Lee Willie's body. His body bolts straight upright, and he grabs the arm of the chair with his left hand. The first surge of electricity comes at 12:07 A.M. It ends ten seconds later but is immediately followed by a jolt of five hundred volts for twenty seconds. Willie's body slumps slightly during this twenty second period. Then, there are another ten seconds of two thousand volts. Willie bolts upright once again. Finally, there are twenty seconds of five hundred volts. Willie's body slumps and never moves again. In all, the electrocution has taken one minute of time. The death chamber is full of smoke. It will take a full five minutes for the air in the room to clear.

After five minutes, Willie's body is finally cool enough for the coroner to touch it without burning his fingers. West Feliciana Parish Coroner Alfred Gould examines Willie and pronounces him dead at 12:15. The door to the witness room opens, and a guard directs us to a table where we stop and sign some papers.

As we go outside, I hear Vern Harvey say, "It was too easy." Later he tells a reporter, "The little jolt of electricity they gave him over there that killed him was just the beginning of the heat that his soul is going to have to put up with for eternity." I leave quickly after the execution, but I hear later that Vern stayed a while outside chatting with reporters. Reportedly, he even asked a female reporter if she would like to dance.

Robert Willie was the thirty-second person executed in the United States since 1977, when the death penalty was re-instituted in this country after a moratorium of five years that resulted from a 1976 decision of the Supreme Court.

Willie was buried in Folsom in his family's cemetery plot after a funeral and a procession to the cemetery of thirty cars. Willie lay in state before the funeral in an open casket, dressed in clothes similar to those in which he was executed: blue jeans and a white tee shirt. Ironically, Faith's funeral had been held at the same funeral home four and a half years earlier. Unlike Willie's open casket, Faith's casket, by necessity, had been closed. During the wake held for Faith at the funeral home, her body had not even been inside the casket. When Faith's body was placed in her casket prior to burial, the Harveys had no choice but to leave her remains unclothed.

The lead story of the ABC evening news with Peter Jennings on Friday, December 28, 1984, was the execution of Robert Willie that had occurred just after midnight earlier that day. It received a total of six minutes of airtime, more than any other story that night. ABC reporter Mark Potter reported on the execution, and his report included statements from Mr. and Mrs. Harvey and their daughter, Lizabeth. Vernon Harvey was shown saying that he wished that the relatives of other victims could witness the execution of the killers of their loved ones. Lizabeth was also shown agreeing that parents of murder victims should be allowed to witness executions. Mrs. Harvey was shown saying that she was glad that Willie would no longer be able to kill others.

Anchor Peter Jennings interviewed Helen Prejean. She said that it was her belief that vengeance is what motivates relatives of victims who wish to witness the execution of the killer. She spoke of her opposition to the death penalty and her desire that it be abolished.

George Will and Peter Jennings then discussed the death penalty and the fact that an overwhelming majority of Americans favor it.

PREJEAN AND PENN

Although Willie and Vaccaro were infamous in southeastern Louisiana in the days and years following the murder of Faith Hathaway, nothing could have prepared them or anyone else for the spotlight that would be thrown on the murder of Faith Hathaway by Sister Helen Prejean, Tim Robbins, Susan Sarandon and Sean Penn.

In 1993, Helen Prejean released her book, *Dead Man Walking: An Eyewitness Account of the Death Penalty in the United States*. It stirred up a lot of bad memories in our community, especially for Vern and Elizabeth Harvey. Still, it was just a ripple in the pond compared to what would happen a couple of years later.

While she was in New Orleans during the filming of John Grisham's *The Client*, Susan Sarandon met Sister Helen Prejean. Later, when Helen Prejean was on a book tour promoting *Dead Man Walking*, Sarandon invited Helen Prejean to visit with her and Tim Robbins at their home. Sarandon also convinced Tim Robbins to make a movie based on the book. As a result, Robbins wrote the screenplay and directed the movie, *Dead Man Walking*, which was released in 1995. The movie was a major commercial success, propelling Susan Sarandon to the top of the Hollywood A-list and earning her an Academy Award for Best Actress.

In the movie, the condemned killer counseled by Helen Prejean, Matthew Poncelet, is portrayed by Sean Penn. He was nominated for an Academy Award for Best Actor for his performance, although he lost to that year's eventual winner, Nicholas Cage.

Matthew Poncelet as portrayed by Sean Penn bears an uncanny resemblance to Robert Lee Willie. Anyone who is familiar with the physical appearance of Robert Lee Willie can clearly see that Matthew Poncelet *is* Robert Lee Willie. It gave me chills when I first saw the movie *Dead Man Walking*. It was almost as if Willie had come back to life. When Sean Penn's character is shown putting his finger to his throat and making a slicing motion, it immediately brought back to my mind the same threatening gesture that Willie had made in court when he saw Mark Brewster, whose throat he had actually cut in a deserted field near Mobile, Alabama.

One of the things I remember most vividly about Robert Lee Willie was the great satisfaction he received from the notoriety his crimes bestowed on him. You could see in his eyes the feeling of grandeur he had from being as "big as Jesse James." I truly believe it was his arrogance and desire for self-aggrandizement that contributed most strongly to his willingness to admit to his role in the murder of Faith Hathaway. He was a sick, evil man who built himself up in his own mind because of the murderous actions he had taken that deprived Faith Hathaway of her then-budding life. If Willie had only known just how renowned he would become after his death, he would have not been able to contain himself.

Still, with all my negative feelings about Sister Prejean, I would probably never have given her much more than a second thought had she not chosen to write of her experiences as spiritual advisor to Elmo Patrick Sonnier and Robert Willie during their last days on Angola's death row. Indeed, after Willie was put to death in 1984, I scarcely thought of Willie and Vaccaro or Helen Prejean until 1993 when the book, *Dead Man Walking*, was published.

Suddenly, once again, all the bad memories came flooding back. The book brought renewed attention to the case of Willie and Vaccaro and on the death penalty itself. In Louisiana, the attention was intense. I was extremely upset that Sister Prejean was glorifying Robert Willie while giving short shrift to the life and grisly death of Faith Hathaway.

Many of Helen Prejean's comments in *Dead Man Walking* shocked and disturbed me greatly. Some of them are simply inaccurate. For example, she says that Willie and Vaccaro took turns raping Debbie in the back seat of Mark's car. This is factually wrong. Robert Willie raped Debbie twice in the car, first when the kidnapping occurred and later at Fricke's Cave after Willie and Vaccaro had left Mark tied to a tree near Mobile, Alabama, with his throat cut and gunshot wounds to his head. Vaccaro did not rape Debbie in Mark's car. He raped Debbie in Tommy Holden's trailer in St. Tammany Parish.

Helen Prejean even gets the name of the town wrong. "Franklington" she calls it. She also refers to the "Franklington Sheriff's Office." Clearly, she is referring to the Washington Parish Sheriff's Office in Franklinton.

More importantly, Helen Prejean fails to indicate as Debbie Morris (Debbie Cuevas's married name) does in her wonderful book, *Forgiving the Dead Man Walking*, that Willie was clearly the leader, that Vaccaro was subservient to the commands of Willie. In fact, Vaccaro told Debbie that it was Willie that demanded that he rape her so that they both would share in the guilt of their crimes against her and Mark.

Sister Prejean says that although Willie acted tough and macho, she can still see the child inside of him. To me, this is outrageous. Helen Prejean has just summarized the horrific crimes committed by Willie that have taken the lives of at least three innocent people and left another physically injured for life. He has deprived a young girl, just starting out on the road to life, of all her dreams, including those of one day being a mother. He has deprived that young girl's parents of their precious child. He has participated in the murder of a police officer that left a widow and young children without a father. And she has the gall to call upon the soft, tender feelings of those who would support Willie and say he's just a little child. Give me a break!

All men were once children. That is too obvious to have to state, but would anyone say, "Oh, Ted Bundy, he's just a little boy inside" or "Poor Jeffrey Dahmer, he was such a nice boy." This kind of niggling little comment is insidious. It sounds innocuous, but it is just like the camel with his nose under the tent. It is the beginning of saying that people shouldn't pay for their crimes because they are not really so bad.

Listen to me. Robert Willie was a man, just as I am, and he had choices to make. Perhaps he did some good things in his life. He may have been kind to his mother when he was little, and I am sure he was a cute baby. But as a man, he chose to take the life of an innocent girl after brutally raping and terrorizing her. In my mind, the child inside Robert Willie no longer existed.

Helen Prejean describes the letter that Willie sends her in reply to her letter offering to meet with him as "pert" and his handwriting as a "tender scrawl." Again, small comments intended to play down the brutality of the man that was Robert Lee Willie. I spent a good deal of time with and around Robert Willie and let me say that "pert" and "tender" are not words that I would use to describe him. You might as well say that Adolph Hitler had twinkling eyes and good handwriting. Both of these might have been true, but they don't change the atrocities committed by him. Neither does a "pert" tone in a letter to a nun or cute handwriting. Let me say that I saw Willie's handwriting on the confession he gave to the murder of Faith Hathaway—a confession in which he talking about "fucking that whore" and neither his handwriting nor his vocabulary impressed me much.

Helen Prejean describes her first meeting with Willie in October 1984, only two months before his execution. She says he was self-possessed and reminded her of a cowboy. Again, she is putting a positive spin on Robert Willie. He was not self-possessed. He was nothing like a cowboy. He was arrogant and crude, evil to the core. The devil himself might display confidence in his bearing. Is this a good thing? To me, it just shows that Willie, arrogant in his crimes, arrogant in his trial, was arrogant to the end.

Remember, his last words were words of pain and arrogance about the murder of Faith Hathaway. He never apologized and said he felt remorse. He didn't say it because he didn't feel remorse. As he said at his second sentencing trial, he was only sorry that he got caught. So while Helen Prejean was admiring Willie for his self-possession and his cowboy bearing, I see in my mind's eye that same old Robert Lee Willie who constantly bummed cigarettes off me in the hallway of the courthouse during his trial. He always knew what he wanted, and he didn't care who stood in his way. It was this same cowboy attribute that resulted in his unfeelingly raping and murdering Faith Hathaway. Some cowboy.

Helen Prejean also describes Willie as "simple and direct." She remarks on how he blew his cigarette smoke down so as not to have it hit her in the face. All in all, she paints a picture of a child-like man, who is polite and tender, simple and direct, he is (she says) "polite, soft-spoken, obviously intelligent"—what is he doing on Death Row? But she did not see the Willie I saw, the Willie that Debbie and Faith Hathaway saw—the real Willie. Take him out of his cage, and he would murder again.

You know, some of what Helen Prejean says is hardly surprising. He was meeting with a nun who had made a special trip to visit him, to be his spiritual advisor, who would fight against the system that was about to take his life as punishment for his horrible crimes. Did she really expect him to have the face of a monster, to spit and snarl at her? The banality of evil, that is what I am reminded of—true evil is banal, plain, unassuming. Again, look at the faces of the most heinous villains of our time—Bundy, Dahmer, Hitler, Gacy. These were the faces of ordinary men, not monsters. But there are monsters among us with the faces of men, and Robert Willie was one of these. He could be polite and nice and all that, but deep down, he was pure evil.

Sister Prejean even has the nerve to imply that "the liquor had lowered Faith's defenses" and that "perhaps it was better that her wits were not so sharp. Better, maybe, for the anesthesia of the alcohol to dull the pain and horror soon to be hers." How dare she say something so cold and unfeeling as this! It is almost as if Faith were being painted as so intoxicated that she did not know what was going on and that she was nearly unconscious during the rape and murder. The evidence was clearly to the contrary. Mel Rose, a bartender at the Lakefront Disco, testified that Faith was not drunk, and even Willie's statements support the truth that Faith was totally aware of the horrors being poured on her. He said, "She will freak out if you don't take her home." This is not the statement he would have made if Faith had been nearly unconscious with alcohol. He also said that she begged Willie and Vacarro to leave and let her die alone. She clearly was in pain and knew her death was imminent. Finally, her wounds included not only many, many stab wounds to the throat and chest, but also defensive wounds that sliced off two of her fingers as she fought and struggled to fend off her attackers. This was not a young woman who was anesthetized and unfeeling of the pain.

Helen Prejean quotes Willie as saying, "I let Joe Vaccaro call all the shots and I went along. I wasn't thinking straight." Maybe Willie said this to Helen Prejean. It certainly is consistent with his long practice of blaming everyone but himself, but the words that Willie spoke were just lies, and her repeating them without questioning them lends support to Willie's story. Read Debbie Morris's book, *Forgiving the Dead Man Walking,* and tell me who was really the leader between Willie and Vaccaro. To Debbie, who was there, it was clearly Willie. To me and everyone else who saw the real Willie and the real Vaccaro, it was clear—Willie was the leader, Vaccaro was the follower. In fact, it was Vaccaro who called the Sheriff's Office during the week of the murder of Faith and the kidnapping of Debbie and Mark and tried to talk about things. He was not the leader. He was under the control of Willie.

Helen Prejean also says that Marion Farmer "had been up against stiff opposition in his bid for re-election at the time of the Hathaway murder." She implies that Marion sought the death penalty against Willie and Vaccaro for political reasons. Helen

Prejean blames the political fallout that occurred in a previous murder case in which Marion permitted the defendants to plead guilty to second-degree murder rather than seek the death penalty. This is simply wrong. First, Marion was not up for re-election at the time of the murder. Second, given the facts of this case, there was no way that anything other than a death penalty case would be made of this.

One of the things that angers me the most about what Helen Prejean says is that she can picture Faith after her death as speaking in opposition to the execution of Robert Lee Willie for her murder because, in death, she knows no hate but only love. In Helen Prejean's vision, Faith does not want the men who murdered her to pay for their crime with their lives. She does go on to say that she can also picture Faith saying that Willie should suffer and die. However, for Helen Prejean to drag Faith back from the grave and to show her voicing support for Helen Prejean's own political view of the world in which murder is never avenged by the killer's own death, where child killers and mass murderers are given a free pass is more than repugnant to me.

One of the funniest things that Helen Prejean says about Willie is that he was sensitive to the body odors of the other Death Row inmates. That might well have been true, but if it was, it was late in coming for Robert Willie. He always had a stench about him. Even Debbie remarked on it in her book, *Forgiving the Dead Man Walking*.

The most outrageous thing that Helen Prejean talks about in *Dead Man Walking* is the position of Faith's body. A couple of days before his execution, Willie is discussing this matter with Helen Prejean, and he says that when he and Vaccaro had finished with Faith, they left her on the floor of Fricke's Cave with her hands on her stomach and her legs down, her knees together.

What a scene! First, brutal rape, then slashing and stabbing with a large Bowie knife, but before you leave your victim, she is all stretched out comfortably with her hands down and her legs together. The only problem is that this is a total lie told by Robert Lee Willie to his spiritual advisor, a person who clearly wanted to believe that the things he told her in his final days were the truth. As the evidence showed at trial, Faith was found with her arms stretched out over her head, her feet up under her and her legs spread as wide apart as humanly possible. The coroner testified that she had died in that position.

Helen Prejean says that there are three explanations: (1) Faith was still alive when Willie and Vaccaro left her bleeding and mutilated in Fricke's Cave and she moved herself into the contorted position in which I found her decomposing body; (2) either I or one of the other law enforcement officers who gathered at the murder scene took Faith's dead arms and moved them over her head and then spread her legs wide apart before crime photographs were taken; or (3) Robert Lee Willie lied when he denied stabbing Faith.

By stating the last possibility, even Helen Prejean apparently recognizes that Willie's story was inherently inconsistent with the physical evidence. Willie said that he was in front of Faith, holding her hands, while Vaccaro was behind Faith with her head in his lap. Vaccaro also said that Willie was in front of Faith. On this point their statements are consistent, and so there is no reason to doubt that Willie was, in fact, positioned in front of Faith at the moment that the murderous attack began. The problem with Willie's statement that he was only holding Faith's hands while Vaccaro repeatedly stabbed her in the throat and chest is that Faith's arms were stretched out over her head. Since Willie was positioned in front of Faith, if he had "merely" been holding her hands down while Vaccaro stabbed her from behind, Willie would have been stretched out over Faith, blocking Vaccaro's clear view of Faith's throat and chest. In other words, the choreography of murder that Willie describes is simply impossible. That means that he was lying about being the one holding Faith's hands. The one standing behind Faith had to have been the one who held her hands down and that was Vaccaro. Willie had to have been the one who stabbed Faith mercilessly while she tried in vain to fend off his attack.

The evidence clearly showed that Faith died in the position in which she was found. There is no doubt about this, and for Helen Prejean to even suggest that Faith was capable or desirous of stretching her arms over her head, putting her feet under her and spreading her legs to the point of breaking apart as she died is ludicrous.

I found Faith's body, and I can testify without a doubt that she was in that position when I found her. Neither I nor anyone else moved her body into that position. You also must remember that when I found Faith's body, she had been dead for a week. Even a casual look at the condition of her body with the decomposition that had occurred shows that her body was not capable of being manipulated into a fake position. Indeed, the maggots formed a clear "chalk-line" around Faith's body, a grisly crime scene outline of the position of her corpse that could not have been staged.

Besides, when Faith's body was first discovered, we had no idea as to the actual facts surrounding her murder. What purpose would moving her body have served us? Finally, her body was extremely fragile. After all the photographs and samples were removed from her body and we finally were cleared to remove her body for transport to the morgue, her head fell off. That leaves only the last possibility: Willie was lying. I could have told Sister Prejean that at the outset if she had asked me.

One of the main things that I notice throughout *Dead Man Walking* is that Helen Prejean seems to blame all of the world's problems on government, but she never once places the blame where it really belongs—on the killers themselves who commit the crimes that send them to Death Row in the first place. For example, Helen Prejean says that free clinics and other welfare programs are not adequately funded mainly because the government spends millions of dollars on executing killers. She should put the blame on murderers for causing the government to be forced to take money from social programs in order to deal with them. Don't blame the government.

Also, throughout *Dead Man Walking*, Helen Prejean tries to

paint law enforcement in the worst light possible. She does not talk about all the thousands of man-hours that law officers spend to protect our communities and to bring dangerous killers to justice. For two straight weeks during the investigation of Faith's murder, I did not sleep more than a couple of hours a night. I gave it everything I had. I did the best I could do. This kind of self-sacrifice is part of the job of a law officer. It goes on every day across this country, but is seldom recognized, particularly by those with a chip on their shoulders because of their opposition to the death penalty.

Helen Prejean quotes Willie as in effect saying that he was deceived into giving his statement in order to protect his mother from prosecution after she was charged for helping him to flee from Louisiana. I did not know much about his mother's case, and I had no axe to grind with Willie's mother. Any mother would probably have helped her son, although mine would have helped me by taking me to the Sheriff's Office. Still, I never promised Willie that his mother would not be prosecuted if he gave a statement. Notice also that Willie does not say that the confession he gave was untrue. Quite the contrary; Robert Lee Willie was bragging when he gave his statement. His statement was the most freely given statement I have ever taken. He loved telling it.

THE DEATH PENALTY

In the United States, the death penalty is an authorized punishment for first-degree murder in thirty-eight of the fifty states. It is also an authorized punishment in the federal courts and in the military. The death penalty is not available in twelve of the states or in the District of Columbia. The United States came close to abolishing the death penalty in this country in its entirety thirty years ago.

In 1972, the United States Supreme Court in the case of *Furman v. Georgia* held that all existing death penalty statutes in the United States were unconstitutional. The problem, according to the Supreme Court, was that juries were given unfettered discretion and were provided with no meaningful guidelines in determining which defendants should be sentenced to death. Significantly, the Supreme Court did not say that the death penalty itself is unconstitutional. Some opponents have long maintained that the death penalty amounts to cruel and unusual punishment in violation of the Eighth Amendment to the United States Constitution. The Supreme Court did not adopt that position in *Furman v. Georgia*. Rather, the Supreme Court determined that in order for the imposition of the death penalty to be proper, the jury that imposes that sentence must have specific guidelines to follow in making that determination of life or death.

Purely from the perspective of the number of persons executed in this country, the Supreme Court's decision in *Furman v. Georgia* changed little. Although it is true that all of the approximately six hundred inmates on death row in 1972 (including the infamous Charles Manson) received an automatic commutation of their sentences from death to life in prison, no one had been executed in the United States since 1967 when convicted murderer Luis Monge was put to death in Colorado's gas chamber.

During the years immediately following the Supreme Court's decision in *Furman v. Georgia*, states worked to draft legislation that would comply with the Court's mandate that juries in capital cases be provided with guidelines in determining the sentences of those convicted. In effect, for a period of four years, from 1972 to 1976, the United States had a Court-sanctioned moratorium on the death penalty.

In 1976, in the case of *Gregg v. Georgia*, the United States Supreme Court held that the newly drafted death penalty statutes in Georgia, Florida and Texas satisfied the requirements of the Constitution in that juries in those states would now be provided with guidelines to follow in deciding whether a particular defendant should be sentenced to death. As a result of the Court's ruling in *Gregg v. Georgia*, first-degree murder trials in which the death penalty is being sought now follow a two-step process. First, a trial is held to determine whether the defendant is guilty or not guilty. Then, if he is found guilty, the same jury determines in a separate hearing whether to impose the death penalty. During the sentencing phase of what is in essence a bifurcated trial, the prosecution presents aggravating circumstances to the jury and the defense presents mitigating circumstances. The focus of the jury is on the particular murder for which the defendant is being tried (i.e., whether it was especially heinous or was committed in connection with the commission of another crime, such as rape or armed robbery) and on the unique characteristics of the defendant himself.

In 1977, Gary Gilmore became the first person in the United States to be executed since 1967 when he was executed by a firing squad in Utah. He was the only person executed that year.

No one was executed in 1978, and only two persons were executed in 1979. Again, no one was executed in 1980 and only one in 1981. Two were executed in 1982, five in 1983, and twenty-one in 1984, the year that Willie was executed. Willie was the thirty-second person executed in the United States since the re-introduction of the death penalty in 1976. As of June 1, 2002, 780 persons have been executed in the United States since the death penalty was re-instituted in 1976. Approximately 3,700 persons are awaiting execution on the nation's Death Rows. The majority of persons executed since 1976 have been white (56.4%) with 34.7% being African-American and 7.2% Hispanic. Whites constitute the largest group on Death Row as well (46%) as compared to 43% for African-Americans and 9% for Hispanics.

Support for and opposition to the death penalty has ebbed and flowed over the years. In 1994, just after the publication of *Dead Man Walking* but before the release of the movie based upon it, support for the death penalty reached an all-time high in the United States—80% according to a Gallup poll. In 2000, support for the death penalty had slipped to 66%, the lowest level in the previous nineteen years. More recently, the trend is in the opposite direction. In May 2002, a Gallup poll showed support for the death penalty in the United States had climbed to 72%, its highest level since 1999. Although, as opponents of the death penalty like to point out, the level of support for the death penalty drops when the poll includes life without parole as an alternative to the death penalty, in a May 2002 Gallup poll, a majority of Americans (52%) still preferred the death penalty over life without parole in cases where such punishments are appropriate.

Still, even though most Americans support the death penalty, the debate over whether it is ever an appropriate punishment continues to rage unabated. As a result of a number of Supreme Court decisions over the years, the death penalty is now reserved only for those convicted of first-degree murder where a jury has determined that there are aggravating circumstances that outweigh whatever mitigating circumstances there may be. Opponents of the death penalty contend, however, that no matter how inhumane or heinous the actions of a killer are, and regardless of the number of his victims or their age or the suffering and torture to which he has subjected them, he should not under any circumstances be punished in any way other than by imprisonment.

What are the arguments against capital punishment that are raised by those who seek its abolition in the United States?

One such argument is that capital punishment is anti-Christian. Helen Prejean makes this argument in *Dead Man Walking*, saying that she simply does not believe that God approves of the death penalty or has granted man the authority to carry out a sentence of death against his fellow man. She notes that Jesus loved those who despised him, and that he accepted the violence of men against him without lashing out in violence himself.

First of all, I want to say that I respect the right of anyone who has a sincere belief that God disapproves of the death penalty to hold to that belief. I don't know anyone else's heart, including Sister Helen Prejean's, but if she or any one else who opposes the death penalty does so because of a heart-felt conviction that it is contrary to the laws of God, then far be it from me to attempt to persuade them to the contrary.

I do know my heart, however. If I believed that God opposed the death penalty, I would also oppose it. It is my firm conviction, however, that the Bible teaches to the contrary—that governments, which are called upon to be fair and just in all their dealings with their citizens, are given the right and the duty to protect those under their care and to punish those who bring death and destruction into their midst.

The Apostle Paul in the letter he wrote to the church in Rome about twenty-five years after the execution of Jesus on the cross said, "Everyone must submit himself to the governing authorities for there is no authority except that which God has established . . . Do you want to be free from fear of the one in authority? Then do what is right and he will commend you. For he is God's servant to do you good. But if you do wrong, be afraid, for he does not bear the sword for nothing. He is God's servant, an agent of wrath to bring punishment on the wrongdoer." (Romans 13:1, 3-4).

Nowhere in the Bible does Jesus make a statement that the death penalty is contrary to the laws of God. Indeed, in the Gospel of Luke, the one thief on the cross who was remorseful and who asked Jesus to remember him said to the other crucified thief, "We are punished justly, for we are getting what our deeds deserve. But this man has done nothing wrong." (Luke 23:41). Jesus is not quoted as disagreeing with the thief nor does Luke comment on the thief's statement. In other words, neither Jesus nor Luke says that the death penalty itself is wrong.

Even death penalty opponents admit that Jesus's statement to the Pharisees who sought to entrap him by asking him whether the woman caught in adultery should be stoned does not lend support for the view that Jesus was making a statement against capital punishment. He said in John 8:7, "If any one of you is without sin, let him be the first to throw a stone at her." By making this statement, Jesus was affirming the Jewish Law of Moses, which called for stoning as the punishment for adultery, while demonstrating the importance of forgiveness and of looking inward at one's own sins before finding fault with others. Jesus was in no way saying, however, that governments do not have the right and authority to punish crime.

One thing that Jesus did say, however, is that he is the life. If anyone will trust in him and turn from his sins, Jesus will be faithful to forgive. I know that I have been forgiven of my sins, and I also know that if Robert Willie asked for forgiveness and trusted Jesus as his Lord and Savior before his death, then Willie's sins were also forgiven, and I will meet him some day in heaven. That is the amazing grace of our God.

From what I have been told and from what I have seen, however, Willie was unrepentant to the end. Instead of using so much of her time railing against the unfairness of the system, it seems to me that Helen Prejean as Willie's spiritual advisor should have focused all of her attention on Robert Lee Willie's soul rather than, as she says in *Dead Man Walking,* "defending Robert Willie's right not to be executed." I think it is no coincidence that Willie's last words— "It makes no difference whether it's citizens, countries, or governments. Killing is wrong."—mirrors so closely Helen Prejean's own words and particularly her disdain for "government."

Another argument raised by opponents of the death penalty, including Helen Prejean, is that the government cannot be trusted to properly operate "the machinery of death." Helen Prejean argues that the death penalty is carried out by a nameless and faceless government that regularly fails in even the simplest day-to-day tasks that it has been entrusted to perform for its citizens and which is often rife with corruption. Hence, in her opinion, governments are simply unworthy of being trusted to determine who should die for his crimes.

In my opinion, this anti-government argument fails on two different levels. First, it fails on a philosophical level. If our state and federal governments are so incompetent, so untrustworthy, so prone to foul-ups that we must scrap the death penalty in its entirety, then why stop there? Surely, if the government is fundamentally incapable of determining which persons accused of first-degree murder actually committed the crimes with which they are charged, then why take a chance on punishing those charged with murder at all? Indeed, why let the government punish anyone?

Second, Helen Prejean's argument fails on a more practical level. That eerily sinister "faceless government" that Sister Prejean fears is nothing more than a boogie man created by those intent on achieving their agenda of abolishing the death penalty. In this country, we *are* the government, and while a government made up of human beings will never be perfect, our system of government is as nearly-perfect as one could hope. Our Constitution and our republic are the products of the collective political genius of our forefathers. It may be true that the "government" cannot always repair a pothole properly, as Helen Prejean jests, but our government has seen us through a revolution, a civil war, two world wars, and numerous other challenges to our freedom, both foreign and domestic. If we lived under a corrupt totalitarian political system, I would probably oppose capital punishment, but not because it would be wrong in and of itself. Rather, I would not trust a corrupt and evil system. As opposed to Helen Prejean, I do trust the rule of law as practiced in the United States of America.

In this regard, it is worth noting that in the United States a person convicted of first-degree murder has an incredible array of protections afforded him to ensure that he will not be deprived of his life without due process of law. Not only are all criminal defendants presumed innocent so that the government must prove them guilty beyond a reasonable doubt, but a conviction requires a unanimous decision by twelve individual citizens who are selected by and questioned by both the government and the defense. Once convicted of first-degree murder, the government must convince a jury to vote unanimously for the death penalty. If a death sentence is imposed, the defendant has multiple layers of appeals, all of which often take more than a decade to complete, and which involve review by state and federal courts, including the United States Supreme Court.

Helen Prejean's argument that the government, this faceless machine, is incapable of doing small things well and so cannot be trusted to do big things well, like determining who should be executed, is a wily argument geared to appeal to most people's inherent distrust in big government. Who hasn't been on the receiving end of a governmental foul-up, from an undeserved tax bill to a parking ticket? It is appealing to most people to throw stones at the big, bad Government with a capital G. If the government is carrying out the death penalty and the government is unfeeling and fraught with errors, it makes sense that we should abolish the death penalty, right?

By that logic, we should abolish all government programs, even those that Helen Prejean favors and about which she complains that President Reagan was cutting in the early 1980's. Perhaps the government should not be trusted to raise armies and defend us either. Let's just go back to living in caves.

Although death penalty opponents have long argued that

innocent men have been put to death, the academic studies that have been done fail to support this argument. Quite simply, there is no credible evidence that a single innocent person has been put to death in the United States in modern times.

On the other hand, there is abundant evidence that the failure to implement the death penalty has resulted in the deaths of numerous innocent people in this country. There are many families today in the United States who grieve for a son or daughter, father or mother, husband or wife who was murdered by an individual who escaped from prison while serving a life sentence for murder or who was paroled after serving only a few years for murder. The lives of prison guards and other inmates are also at risk from those murderers sentenced to life in prison rather than to death for their crimes. It is not that uncommon to pick up a newspaper and read of a killing inside a prison by a man already serving a life sentence for murder. Had this man been sentenced to death and executed, the life of the prison guard or the other inmate would have been spared.

Helen Prejean also argues that capital punishment constitutes mental torture of the inmate awaiting death because he is told he is going to be executed and then held prisoner for a long time with the knowledge of his scheduled death, which is often postponed at the very last moment, adding even more psychological stress to the condemned prisoner. She believes that capital punishment is little different than murder. In effect, she appears to believe that Robert Lee Willie's multiple stabbing and near decapitation of Faith Hathaway was no greater crime than the state-ordered execution of Willie in the electric chair. Helen Prejean even subscribes to the view of the late French writer and philosopher Albert Camus that capital punishment renders the government in some ways more inhuman and monstrous than the murderer it is seeking to execute.

I believe that any attempt to equate the act of murder to the action of the State in enforcing the death penalty is simple-minded and insulting to the surviving family members of murder victims. When one person intentionally takes the life of another person who is innocent and undeserving of death, that is a criminal act of the highest order. We call that murder.

On the other hand, when a person is sentenced to death unanimously by a jury and then has his conviction and sentence reviewed and upheld by court after court after court before being put to death, that is not murder. That is not the taking of innocent life. That is the imposition of punishment.

Opponents of the death penalty, however, do not believe that we have the right to punish those who have committed the most horrific and heinous of murders by executing them. Helen Prejean has said that she believes that all persons have the fundamental right not to be killed. According to Helen Prejean, killing is wrong in all its forms, whether individuals in the commission of unspeakable violence on other individuals carry it out or whether it is carried out under color of law and in accordance with strictly followed guidelines by states or the federal government.

I believe that innocent people have a right not to be killed. I believe that we as a society have a right to protect ourselves from those who would kill us by executing those among us who have shown that they endanger us all by their freely chosen acts of premeditated murder. I believe that we have the collective right to put to death those individuals whose murderous actions merit the ultimate punishment.

Helen Prejean says that all men have equivalent moral worth, and so there is no basis for depriving one man of his life in our society. This is simply not true. In this society, we all have equal rights, but there are people who have more worth than others. Were this not true, we would not incarcerate violent felons. Robert Willie and Joe Vaccaro committed unspeakable acts of violence and depravity on an innocent eighteen-year-old girl. To say that their lives have an equal worth in our society after their freely committed acts of violence demeans all of us, most particularly Faith Hathaway.

Helen Prejean argues that the death penalty inflicts psychological torture and that the death penalty is more extreme psychic violence than any human being inflicts on another. This argument, to me, is frivolous. Perhaps, it is too much for the sensitive temperament of the murderer to be put to the trouble of standing trial. The tension and anxiety that must accompany being publicly accused of first-degree murder must produce a sleepless night in jail for the occasional defendant with some semblance of a conscience. How embarrassing to have his evil acts recounted in public, even talked about on television and in the newspapers! Surely, we can all do away with the needless assault on the sensibilities of our criminal citizens. After all, we are all equal in worth. Right?

If you follow this argument to its logical conclusion, then a lifetime of imprisonment must also qualify as torture, and so disqualify its use for punishing crime. We would be left with imposing minor fines and monetary penalties for murder, perhaps requiring murderers to pick up trash on the sides of roads.

Helen Prejean argues that the death penalty is not a deterrent to future acts of murder. She goes so far to say that it is incontrovertible that there is no deterrent effect to the death penalty.

The truth is that there are conflicting studies on the deterrent effect of the death penalty. Opponents of the death penalty can cite studies that lend support for the proposition that there is no deterrent effect; proponents can cite other studies. However, academic studies and statistical analyses paint a broad picture. We're talking about life and death when we discuss the death penalty—not just the life or death of the person convicted of murder, but the life or death of future innocent victims of crime. I challenge any opponent of the death penalty who is willing to be honest with himself or herself to answer this one question: Can you truthfully say that you do not believe that the possibility of the death penalty has ever prevented the commission of even one single murder? If the death penalty has prevented the death of even one innocent person, its deterrent effect is a factor in its favor. Personally, I believe that the fear of possible execution has prevented the commission of many murders.

Still, however, whether the death penalty is a deterrent or not is of limited significance to me. I do not support the death penalty because of its deterrent effect. I support the death penalty because it is just. When an individual commits a murder of such barbarity and cruelty that only the ultimate retribution satisfies the demand of justice, then we should have the right and authority to impose the death penalty.

Opponents of the death penalty argue that we can punish those convicted of the worst offenses adequately and protect society by imposing true life sentences—life without the possibility of parole. I still maintain that justice sometimes demands more than long-term imprisonment in retribution for certain crimes. However, even if incapacitating the worst of the convicted first-degree murderers were appropriate, we can never incapacitate perfectly with imprisonment. Inmates serving life sentences kill guards and other prisoners. And murderers serving life sentences sometimes escape. Even such a high-profile inmate as James Earl Ray, the convicted killer of Dr. Martin Luther King, escaped from prison and was on the loose for three days. In 1984, five Death Row inmates escaped from a Virginia prison and were not recaptured for nineteen days. One of the escapees had raped and killed a woman who was eight months pregnant along with her five-year-old son. Does anyone doubt that he or one of the other escapees would have killed again if they had not been recaptured? Murderers serving life sentences have also escaped from prisons in Utah and New Jersey. The only way to be certain that innocent people will not be victimized by those already convicted of the worst crimes is to carry out the death penalty.

But what about forgiveness, some might say? What part does mercy play? I believe that God is merciful. If a Death Row inmate asks God to forgive him, he will be forgiven. In God's eyes, it will be as though he had never committed the crime for which he is on Death Row. God says that as far as the east is from the west, he will remove our sin and remember it no more. However, God does not turn back the hands of time when he forgives. We are responsible for our actions, and, in this world, we have to bear the consequences of our bad choices and evil actions.

EPILOGUE

So much has happened in the more than twenty years since Faith Hathaway was ripped from the streets of Mandeville, Louisiana, and murdered in the remote woods of Fricke's Cave. The world that Faith knew, that Robert Willie knew, has changed so much. For many of the people whose lives were touched by the murderous actions of Robert Willie and Joe Vaccaro, life now is very much a continuing result of the actions that took place so long ago.

Debbie Morris (the former Debbie Cuevas) is married and has a beautiful family. Debbie is involved in Christian activities and speaks candidly about her terrible ordeal. In 1996, she published a book detailing the crimes committed against her and Mark Brewster and how she has come to forgive Robert Lee Willie and Joe Vaccaro. Debbie's book is entitled *Forgiving the Dead Man Walking*. After her book was published, Debbie wrote me a note and sent me a copy of her book. She said that I was at the top of the list of the few law enforcement people who stood out in their concern for her. She said she could tell that I personally felt the grief and the horror of the things that had happened as a result of the actions of Willie and Vaccaro.

Mark Brewster works today as a mechanic for the state of Louisiana on the Lake Pontchartrain Causeway, just across the bridge from where the bloody rampage of Willie and Vaccaro took place in the quiet towns of Mandeville and Madisonville two decades ago.

Vernon and Elizabeth Harvey became public advocates of the death penalty in the years following the murder of their daughter. They attended all executions held at Angola to show their support for the families of murder victims. Occasionally, they would bring Faith's younger half-sister, Lizabeth, with them.

Vernon Harvey died on Sunday, April 28, 1996, at the age of sixty-nine, as a result of a heart attack in his home in Mandeville. Elizabeth Harvey is still going strong. She lives in Mandeville and still attends executions at Angola whenever they occur. Elizabeth Harvey has also become very active in Victims and Citizens Against Crime, an advocacy and support group for the families of victims of violent crime that is headquartered in New Orleans, and that has a great deal of influence in the judicial and penal system in Louisiana. She also serves as a member of the Crime Victims Reparations Board, which is a part of the Louisiana Commission on Law Enforcement.

In 1994, a newborn baby girl was found washed up on the shores of Lake Pontchartrain south of Slidell not far from the place where Faith was kidnapped. When she was found, the umbilical cord and part of the placenta were still attached. An autopsy confirmed that the baby girl was dead before she had been placed adrift in the dark waters of Lake Pontchartrain. Although her true name and identity was never discovered, she was simply called Baby Hope. Elizabeth Harvey took Baby Hope and had her buried in her family's cemetery plot, alongside the remains of her daughter, Faith.

In 1982, Judge Crain was elevated from the trial court to Louisiana's First Circuit Court of Appeals. Judge Crain has retired from the bench, although he now serves as the chairman of the Louisiana Gaming Control Board. Judge James has also retired from the bench.

All of the principal lawyers involved in the case are still practicing law. Bill Alford is a prominent defense lawyer who often defends those accused of serious crime, including murder. "Mike," Bill said, "it's a lot different defending people charged with murder than it was when I was prosecuting them. Now, I get to know them a lot better and have realized that everyone, no matter how heinous their crime, has a little good in them."

"What good were you able to find in Willie?" I ask.

"I didn't spend very much time with him," Bill said. "So, honestly I didn't find any."

Herb Alexander bought a copy of *Dead Man Walking* directly from Helen Prejean. He autographed it: "To Mike Varnado, the best damn investigator there ever was" and gave the book to me.

Marion Farmer has an office in Covington and has a general practice of law.

Austin McElroy is practicing law in St. Tammany Parish after several years of practicing civil and criminal law in New York. He has said that Willie was "cocky as hell." He also said that Willie was never cooperative with him in preparing his defense, and that he was a "totally amoral person." "I got the impression he wanted to be convicted so he would be the big man on campus," he said. "He wanted to see all the newspaper clippings. He knew exactly what he was doing and what was going on."

After Willie was convicted, Austin said that Willie did not want to appeal anything because Willie was under the impression that his federal life sentences would protect him. Asked for his personal opinion of who actually stabbed Faith Hathaway, Austin said that he thinks that Willie did the actual stabbing.

Austin said that Willie did not want to testify at his original trial, and that he really did not want his mother or his aunt to testify either. Austin said that he saw the trailers for the movie *Dead Man Walking* and Sean Penn looked so much like Robert Lee Willie that he wanted nothing to do with the movie.

During the trial, someone trashed Austin's front lawn and broke the window on his car. Even though he was Robert Lee Willie's lawyer, he said that the Harveys were always polite and nice to him.

Tommy Holden is dead. He was found hanged on his front porch, although I believe that his death was not a result of suicide.

Joe Vaccaro is in a federal prison in Florence, Colorado. In June 1990, Joe Vaccaro wrote to *The Daily News* in Bogalusa and to the ACLU, claiming that he and not Willie had stabbed and killed

Faith Hathaway. He claimed that he had documented evidence that Willie had not been the actual killer. He even went so far as to say that Willie had nothing to do with Faith's death. In capital letters that were underlined in red, Vaccaro said, "It's a tragedy that someone died for something he didn't do."

In his 1990 letter, Vaccaro claimed that he and Willie had picked Faith up at 4:30 in the morning while she was hitchhiking. He said that when he offered LSD to Faith, she said that she had never done drugs before, but since it was her last night of freedom before joining the Army, she would try it.

Vaccaro also said that he asked Faith for sex when they got to Fricke's Cave, and she agreed willingly. Accordingly to Vaccaro, they left Willie in the truck and walked down into the Cave. He said that after Faith had taken off her pants and laid down on them, he looked back to see if Willie could see them. When he looked back at Faith, she no longer looked like herself. Rather, she had a head like a goat and legs like a deer and wings on her back. Vaccaro blamed this alleged hallucination on the LSD he had been taking.

He said that all he could think to do was kill Faith. He said he stabbed her two or three times and then she looked like Faith again, but only momentarily before changing back to the creature. He continued to stab her until she was dead. Vaccaro claimed that Willie was in the truck the whole time this was going on.

Vaccaro's claims were met with a healthy dose of skepticism. Even one of his former defense attorneys, Tom Ford, said that Vaccaro was lying. Since Vaccaro had already been sentenced to multiple life sentences, he had nothing to lose by claiming full credit for Faith's murder. Potentially, he had something to gain from his assertions. For example, he could help out his friends on Death Row by throwing doubt on the accuracy of the proceedings in his case. Ford said that Vaccaro could be saying all of this just to win himself a trip home in the event local authorities wished to investigate this matter further.

One of the jurors on Robert Willie's second sentencing jury who asked to remain anonymous recently told me that she did not register to vote until about three or four years ago because she was afraid she would be called to serve on another jury. She said that she could not believe someone could be as evil as Robert Lee Willie. She had to seek counseling from her pastor after serving on the jury. Usually, Willie kept his eyes down, she said, but every once in a while, he would look at each juror individually, going down the row, person by person, "almost as if he were looking down into your soul." She was surprised by how small he was, not physically intimidating at all. When he testified, he was mean and hard and had a hateful attitude. When I spoke with her, she cried when she talked about how the members of the jury passed the knife and Faith's shirt around among the jurors.

As for me, the years following the death of Faith were among the toughest years of my life. A job I once loved, one that I couldn't believe I was getting paid to do, turned into perfect dread. I found myself drinking and taking painkillers to hide from my past experiences and my present responsibilities. Indeed, days would go by without my even leaving the house, much less exposing myself to the daily grind at the District Attorney's Office. I found myself drinking more and more each night in an effort to sleep. It would be years later before I realized that what had been missing in my life could not be found at the bottom of a bottle of whiskey nor could it be found in a packet of pills. The answers that I was searching for and missing were closer than the liquor store; they were much closer than the pharmacy. All the time the answers were within a foot or two of my bed, lying dusty on my lamp table there. My Bible.

I learned volumes about how victims should be treated by working on this case. Unfortunately, I know that I made a lot of mistakes in dealing with Vern and Elizabeth Harvey. I should have recognized that the Harveys were merely grasping for all the information they could get in an effort to glean even the smallest piece of sanity from an insane and ruthless act. Now that I am older and have children of my own around the same age as young Faith was when she was butchered, I understand their hunger for knowledge about the crime much better now. I was only twenty-five years old when I found Faith's body and while leading the investigation, and I was truly too green and insensitive to understand the desperate parental obsession from the Harveys, as when they wanted to look at the horrible crime scene photographs. It was not until years later that I fully came to understand this request.

Now I have not only learned that a victim's innocent parents have a right to see any and all of the information the authorities have available, I have learned that it is also the prudent thing for a homicide investigator to do. Why? Because the parents have exactly the same goal as the investigators—simply put, to catch and bring to justice the killers. An investigator can find no better source of information than the parents of a murdered child.

I was very insensitive to victims and their families until I became involved in the investigation of Faith's murder. I was not trained by anyone to show compassion for the victims or the families. This case changed all that. Thanks to Elizabeth and Vern and to my own mother's suffering as a result of the loss of one of my brothers to homicide in September 1979, I have become acutely aware of the anguish of the family members of murder victims. In a way, my heightened ability to empathize with a victim's family has been a curse to me emotionally, because I now know how much unimaginable suffering goes on when something like this happens. Now when I see a dead, murdered body, I do not merely see a corpse—I see someone's brother, sister, child, father or mother lying there. Not some piece of evidence.

I now know why most of the older detectives never considered the victims and their families. To humanize the victims and families was probably too painful to them. You are supposed to get "hardened" after working these cases over the years. It became worse and worse for me. The suffering of victims' loved ones made me work a lot harder on these kinds of things, because I knew that if the killer was not caught and brought to justice, the family would suffer much more. I was scared to death that I would get a case some day that I could not solve. Before Faith's murder, even though I wanted to catch every killer, it was more like a game. Afterwards, I was desperate to get it done. This caused a lot of problems, not only for my health, but also in my relationships with family and friends. I became like a madman. I could not think about anything else. I could not hear when my kids were talking to me, when I came home for thirty minutes to see them. It was so strong in my mind that no matter what I did, I could not get away from it until it was over. Not even for a minute. I even dreamed about it when I slept for a few hours. It was terrible. When it was over and everybody was patting me on the back, all I could think about was what was going to happen next. I did not even get the satisfaction of a job done well. I was thinking about how I could have solved it quicker. Did I do anything that was going to cause me problems in court? What was I going to say to the family? I could not enjoy the "game" anymore since I had been enlightened to the suffering of the victim.

In 1996, I was contacted by Elizabeth Harvey and asked to give an interview to PBS about the murder of Faith Hathaway. At first I was very reluctant. I wanted to put this case behind me. Also, I was afraid that PBS was looking for a way to promote Sister Prejean and her campaign to abolish the death penalty. After all, this was just after the phenomenal success of the movie *Dead Man Walking*. However, after talking to the two producers of the documentary that was planned, Chris Buchanan and Ben Loeterman, I was convinced that the documentary would be a balanced effort. I was not disappointed.

The PBS Frontline episode, *Angel on Death Row*, aired on April 9, 1996. That night, my phone rang off the hook until I unplugged it at midnight. The next day, the phone at work rang off the hook as well. My State Representative, Dr. Jerry Thomas, who had been the coroner when Faith was murdered, mentioned *Angel on Death Row* while at the legislature just a few days afterwards. Another state legislator came up to me and introduced himself, telling me what Jerry had said about me to the other senators and representatives. The sheriff also told me that dozens of legislators came up to him complimenting the office about how professional we were. He came to my house from the legislature to get a copy of the PBS documentary. He told me later that he has never been prouder of one of his deputies. My high school English teacher came to the Sheriff's Office and also told me how proud she was. She had not seen me in twenty-five years! Walking down the street just after Faith's murder, I would have people cross the street to shake my hand. People I did not even know. I would hear people whispering when standing in line. They would say things like, "Look, that's the investigator." After the movie *Dead Man Walking* and the PBS documentary, it started all over. It really has never stopped. I run into ten to fifteen people whom I do not know every year who want to shake my hand.

Angel on Death Row won an Emmy Award for Best Documentary. In a letter to me from Christopher Buchanan, Associate Producer of Frontline, dated March 21, 1996, Chris said, "It goes without saying that I wish all cops were as easy to work with, but you've gone way beyond that benchmark. Your patience, your candor and honesty, and your diligence are all greatly appreciated by Ben and myself. Although we could have told 'the other half' of the story without you, it wouldn't have been nearly as easy nor more importantly as good." The following year the Rotary Club in Bogalusa and the Kiwanis Club in Franklinton named me deputy of the year.

Looking back, I know now that I made a mess of my first attempt to talk to Mark Brewster at the trial, talking to him in a loud voice as if he were deaf. I was horribly embarrassed by my failure to reach out better to Mark. I did not give it a second try until PBS wanted me to speak to him. I went to the Causeway Police Mechanic's Shop where he worked and walked up to him. I introduced myself to Mark, telling him who I was. He looked at me and smiled a little, and said, "Mr. Mike, I know who you are." Again I felt stupid. He was very polite. I did not put him on the spot. I gave him the names of the PBS producers and a telephone number and told him if he would like to tell his story that I wanted him to have an opportunity. If he did not want to get involved with the documentary, I in no way wanted him to. I explained that it was his decision and his alone. I shook his hand and left. Mark is a very handsome and well-mannered man. I was very pleased that he showed no outward signs of the horrendous ordeal that he went through at the hands of Willie and Vaccaro. I felt better about everything after I saw him.

Debbie Morris told me that she had seen me several times in Covington while she was working as a waitress, but did not dare approach me because I looked like I was too busy, and she did not want to make me feel uncomfortable. It's funny how young people act. I saw her at the same times, but I thought it might make her uncomfortable if I approached her. I did not want to do anything that might make all the bad memories come back. I thought I might be part of those bad memories. Only years later did I find out she wanted to speak to me but was somehow afraid. When I was participating in a documentary for Dutch television that Debbie was doing after her book, *Forgiving the Dead Man Walking*, came out, she listened to what I said during the interview. She told me that I shared exactly the same views as her father. She said I caused her to rethink her position again. When we parted I told her that her husband and children were very lucky indeed to have somebody like her. I meant it.

Until only a few months ago, I continued my work as a detective with the Washington Parish Sheriff's Office. After twenty-six years of working in the criminal justice system as an investigator, sixteen of those years in law enforcement, I finally retired from law enforcement earlier this year.

I now enjoy the freedom of working for myself as a private investigator in Washington and St. Tammany parishes. My best times now are spent with my family, particularly my two sons, making up for missed time. Truly, as my mother has always told me, "The Good Lord closes some doors only to open others."

In a letter dated January 21, 1996, Helen Prejean wrote to Vern and Elizabeth Harvey, expressing regret that the release of the film *Dead Man Walking* had been painful to them. She suggested that the Harveys see the film and give it a chance, saying that it presented the victim's side of the death penalty issue in a respectful way. She told Mrs. Harvey that she hoped they could remain friends, although she would understand if Mrs. Harvey felt that this was impossible. Helen Prejean said that she would try to get at least $5,000 of the proceeds from the film to the Harveys, but she cautioned that her Order, the Sisters of St. Joseph, would have the final say on that since they were the recipients of money from the film and not her personally. As of today, over six years later, Mrs. Harvey has never received a penny from the proceeds of the film.

Sister Helen Prejean has achieved worldwide fame as a result of her book *Dead Man Walking* and the movie based on it. She has been nominated for the Nobel Peace Prize four times since the publication of *Dead Man Walking*, which itself was nominated for a Pulitzer Prize. On Saturday, October 7, 2000, an opera based on the *Dead Man Walking* movie premiered in San Francisco.

Today, Helen Prejean is the driving force behind the Moratorium Campaign, a worldwide movement to stop executions. It has been reported that Sister Prejean is planning to release a new book in the next few months about several Death Row inmates who, she claims, are innocent. If so, I have little doubt that the spotlight will be focused even more intently than at present on the death penalty, although I will be surprised if the victims of crime and their families will get much press.

Meanwhile, Faith Hathaway's earthly remains lie buried beneath the smooth gravel of a modest cemetery plot in a remote corner of a small graveyard in Mandeville, Louisiana, her name hardly known. On the weekend of what would have been Faith's twentieth high school reunion, her sister, Lizabeth, went to visit Faith's grave. There, she found a small note that had been written by three girls who were classmates of Faith at Mandeville High School. The note read, "Dear Faith, We remember. We were all out together the night you died. You said to me, 'If I never see you again, have a good life.' We'll have good lives, Faith. We wish you peace."

With all my heart, I do as well.